★ World War II ★

STRATEGIC BATTLES IN EUROPE

by Earle Rice Jr.

Lucent Books, P.O. Box 289011, San Diego, CA 92198-9011

Titles in The American War Library series include:

World War II
Hitler and the Nazis
Kamikazes
Leaders and Generals
Life as a POW
Life of an American Soldier in
  Europe
Strategic Battles in Europe
Strategic Battles in the Pacific
The War at Home
Weapons of War

The Civil War
Leaders of the North and South
Life Among the Soldiers and
  Cavalry
Lincoln and the Abolition of
  Slavery
Strategic Battles
Weapons of War

Library of Congress Cataloging-in-Publication Data

Rice, Earle, Jr.
    Strategic battles in Europe / by Earle Rice Jr.
      p.   cm.—(The American war library series)
    Includes bibliographical references and index.
    Summary: Discusses strategic battles in Europe during
World War II, including Operation Torch, Operation Husky,
the Italian Campaign, Operation Overlord, the Battle of the Bulge,
last battles, and VE Day.
    ISBN 1-56006-536-2 (lib. bdg. : alk. paper)
    1. World War, 1939–1945—Juvenile literature. 2. Battles—
History—20th century—Juvenile literature. [1. World War,
1939–1945—Campaigns—Europe.] I. Title. II. Series
D743.7.H46 2000
940.53—dc21   99-031358
                                                            CIP

Printed in the U.S.A.

★ Contents ★

A Nation Forged by War

The United States, like many nations, was forged and defined by war. Despite Benjamin Franklin's opinion that "There never was a good war or a bad peace," the United States owes its very existence to the War of Independence, one to which Franklin wholeheartedly subscribed. The country forged by war in 1776 was tempered and made stronger by the Civil War in the 1860s.

The Texas Revolution, the Mexican-American War, and the Spanish-American War expanded the country's borders and gave it overseas possessions. These wars made the United States a world power, but this status came with a price, as the nation became a key but reluctant player in both World War I and World War II.

Each successive war further defined the country's role on the world stage. Following World War II, U.S. foreign policy redefined itself to focus on the role of defender, not only of the freedom of its own citizens, but also of the freedom of people everywhere. During the cold war that followed World War II until the collapse of the Soviet Union, defending the world meant fighting communism. This goal, manifested in the Korean and Vietnam conflicts, proved elusive, and soured the American public on its achievability. As the United States emerged as the world's sole superpower, American foreign policy has been guided less by national interest and more on protecting international human rights. But as involvement in Somalia and Kosovo prove, this goal has been equally elusive.

As a result, the country's view of itself changed. Bolstered by victories in World Wars I and II, Americans first relished the role of protector. But, as war followed war in a seemingly endless procession, Americans began to doubt their leaders, their motives, and themselves. The Vietnam War especially caused people to question the validity of sending its young people to die in places where they were not particularly wanted and for people who did not seem especially grateful.

While the most obvious changes brought about by America's wars have been geopolitical in nature, many other aspects of society have been touched. War often does not bring about change directly, but acts instead like the catalyst in a chemical reaction, accelerating changes already in progress.

Some of these changes have been societal. The role of women in the United States had been slowly changing, but World War II put thousands into the workforce and into uniform. They might have gone back to being housewives after the war, but equality, once experienced, would not be forgotten.

Likewise, wars have accelerated technological change. The necessity for faster airplanes and a more destructive bomb led to the development of jet planes and nuclear energy. Artificial fibers developed for parachutes in the 1940s were used in the clothing of the 1950s.

Lucent Books' American War Library covers key wars in the development of the nation. Each war is covered in several volumes, to allow for more detail, context, and to provide volumes on often neglected subjects, such as the kamikazes of World War II, or weapons used in the Civil War. As with all Lucent Books, notes, annotated bibliographies, and appendixes such as glossaries give students a launching point for further research. In addition, sidebars and archival photographs enhance the text. Together, each volume in The American War Library will aid students in understanding how America's wars have shaped and changed its politics, economics, and society.

Selection of Battles

This book is about the major battles fought by Americans and their allies in the European and Mediterranean Theaters during World War II. The term *battle*, when applied to each of the six major engagements selected for inclusion herein, should be interpreted in the sense of an extended struggle rather than as a fleeting clash of arms.

For the American soldier—or GI (from "government issue")—at the time of the U.S. entry into World War II, the road to Berlin coursed first through North Africa, then, successively, through Sicily, Italy, Normandy, across the Rhine, and through the heartland of Germany. Thus, the battles, or campaigns, portrayed in the subsequent chapters reflect a representative sampling of every turn in the road, namely, the Battle for North Africa, the Battle for Sicily, Salerno-Anzio-Rapido, the Normandy landings, the Battle of the Bulge, and Remagen and the race to Berlin.

Except for the Battle of the Bulge—Adolf Hitler's last-gasp offensive in the forested Ardennes region of Belgium, Luxembourg, and France—these choices represent prolonged, full-scale Allied offensive actions. Taken together, their objectives and time frames provide an outline of Allied strategy and stake chronological signposts along the bloody road to Berlin.

During Operation Torch, or the Battle for North Africa (8 November 1942–13 May 1943), for example, the American GI entered into the rigors and horrors of war across the Atlantic for the first time. When pitted against the elite troops of German field marshal Erwin Rommel's Afrika Korps at Kasserine Pass, he experienced the humiliation of defeat. But under new, determined leadership, he redeemed himself and played a vital role in driving the Germans out of North Africa and forcing Germany finally on the defensive. After Kasserine Pass, Lieutenant General Dwight D. Eisenhower said that his GIs were "mad and ready to fight."[1]

Military Twenty-Four-Hour Clock

Military times are used throughout the book. This key, showing familiar A.M. and P.M. times paired with the corresponding time on the twenty-four-hour clock, may be helpful in learning the system.

A.M.	24	P.M.	24
1	0100	1	1300
2	0200	2	1400
3	0300	3	1500
4	0400	4	1600
5	0500	5	1700
6	0600	6	1800
7	0700	7	1900
8	0800	8	2000
9	0900	9	2100
10	1000	10	2200
11	1100	11	2300
12	1200	12	2400

Using North Africa as a springboard to invade the soft underside of Europe, the Allies launched the battle for Sicily, code-named Operation Husky (10 July–17 August 1943). Of Husky, corps commander Major General Omar N. Bradley said, "Seldom in war has a major operation been undertaken in such a fog of indecision, confusion and conflicting plans."[2] Yet in little more than a month, the U.S. 7th Army and the British 8th Army drove the Germans off the large Italian island and forced the surrender of the Italian army. Italy now lay within their easy traverse across the narrow Strait of Messina.

In Operation Avalanche, the invasion of Salerno (9–18 September 1943), the U.S. 5th Army, along with U.S. rangers and British commandos, established a beachhead preparatory to driving on the key port city of Naples, twenty-five miles to the north. On the evening of 16 September, U.S. lieutenant general Mark Clark reported to General Eisenhower, "I am prepared to attack Naples."[3] Naples fell on 1 October 1943, providing the Allies with a vital supply base for their drive up the Italian boot toward Rome.

The fighting in Italy continued, and the Allied advance on Rome became blocked at the "Winter Line" (Gustav-Cassino Line) in late 1943. A daring attempt by American and British allies to outflank the Germans at Anzio, thirty miles south of Rome, commenced on 22 January 1944. This attempt, dubbed Operation Shingle, nearly met with disaster.

During Operation Avalanche, British commandos watch as an American ship lays down a smoke screen at Salerno. The Allies would soon advance toward Rome.

The Germans surrounded the Allied beachhead and threatened to shove the invaders back into the sea. But the Allies hung on doggedly. A stalemate soon developed that lasted until the Allies began a successful breakout on 23 May. Rome became the first Axis capital to fall on 4 June 1944. The Normandy landings began a day and a half later.

Operation Overlord, the long-awaited invasion to establish a second front in Western Europe, got under way on 6 June 1944—D day. The invasion force constituted the largest assemblage of ships, planes, and troops ever assembled for an amphibious operation. Soviet leader Joseph Stalin, commenting on the opera-

tion, said, "The history of wars does not know any such undertaking so broad in conception and so grandiose in scale and so masterly in execution."[4] In reality, the execution of the undertaking fell considerably short of perfection, but it did succeed.

By 20 June, the Allies had put a million men ashore. The long, arduous task of driving the Nazis out of Western Europe had begun.

Six months later, the Allied armies stood poised along Germany's western border, temporarily stalled by the stout defenses of the German Siegfried Line but still holding the initiative.

Early on 16 December, under a blanket of dense fog, the Germans struck suddenly along an eighty-five-mile front in the Ardennes. In an audacious offensive conceived and planned by Hitler himself, the Germans hoped to split the Allied forces in a drive intended to carry all the way to Antwerp. Of Hitler's brainstorm, Field Marshal Walther Model, commander of

In the largest amphibious operation ever undertaken, troops and equipment stream ashore at Normandy.

German Army Group B, said, "This plan hasn't got a damned leg to stand on."[5]

Nonetheless, Hitler's Ardennes Offensive, also known as the Battle of the Bulge, (16 December 1944–28 January 1945), came close to succeeding. It was stopped primarily because of the ingenuity, skill, and courage of the American GI, who by then had become a deadly fighter. The battle delayed the Allied timetable by at least a month. But German losses further weakened their ability to stem the advancing tide of Allied armies.

To the amazement of the first elements of the U.S. 9th Armored Division to reach the Ludendorff Railway Bridge in Rema-

gen, Germany, they found it still standing and spanning the Rhine River on 7 March 1945. The Allies had expected to find the Remagen Bridge, as it was popularly known, blown up by the withdrawing German armies. When General Omar Bradley requested permission to cross over it into the Rhineland, an operations officer in Supreme Headquarters scoffed and said, "You've got a bridge, but it's in the wrong place. It just doesn't fit the plan."[6]

Bradley's GIs reshaped the plan and crossed over the bridge. By nightfall, they had established a rapidly expanding

An infantryman stands guard over German soldiers captured at the Battle of the Bulge. The ingenuity, skill, and courage of the American GI stopped Hitler's offensive.

bridgehead on the east bank of the Rhine, thereby opening the way for the Allied advance deep into Germany.

Meanwhile, Soviet armies on the eastern front were pressing closer to the German capital. Allied and Axis combatants positioned themselves for the last battles of the war in Europe. The race to Berlin was on.

Chapter 1

World War II in Europe

"You may strip Germany of her colonies, reduce her armaments to a mere police force and her navy to that of a fifth-rate power; all the same, in the end, if she feels that she has been unjustly treated in the peace of 1919, she will find means of exacting retribution from her conquerors."
—David Lloyd George, British prime minister, 25 March 1919
(quoted in Robert Leckie, *The Wars of America*)

When the root causes of World War II are sifted and reduced to the actions of a single individual, few analysts would deny that the one person most responsible for the greatest war in human history was Adolf Hitler.

Hitler, a former corporal in the German army during World War I, rose to supreme power in Germany on policies of hate and deceit. Spewing hatred for Communists and Jews, and promising to restore a humiliated Germany to its former status as a world-class power, he won the support of workers, bankers, and industrialists. Hitler was appointed chancellor of Germany on 30 January 1933 and embarked on a treacherous political and militaristic path aimed at leading Germany to world domination.

In March 1935, the new chancellor—the Führer (leader)—publicly rejected the Versailles Treaty, in particular its restrictions on German military strength. He began rebuilding the Luftwaffe (air force) and developed a new form of panzer (tank) warfare.

In the pursuit of lebensraum (living space), Hitler reacquired territories stripped from Germany at Versailles—and acquired even more—in a succession of bluff moves. These included the Rhineland, Austria, the Sudetenland, Bohemia and Moravia, and Memel.

On 23 August 1939, Hitler shocked Europe and the world by signing a nonaggression pact with the Soviet Union. Known as the Hitler-Stalin Pact, it contained secret clauses for partitioning Poland between the signatory nations. This alliance between avowed enemies represented another stunning coup for the German dictator. "Now," Hitler proclaimed, "I have the world in my pocket."[7]

On 1 September 1939, Hitler sent his armies racing into Poland. Spearheaded by tanks and planes, they introduced a fearful world to the blitzkrieg, or lightning war.

Two days later, Britain and France declared war on Germany. Britain immediately announced a sea blockade against Germany, as it had done in World War I. But this was a new kind of war.

The blitzkrieg begins. On 1 September 1939, Hitler sent his troops storming into Poland accompanied by tanks and planes.

Britain Fights On

Britain and France could not stop Hitler's juggernaut from rolling over Poland in four weeks. The Red Army hastened Poland's collapse, entering into eastern Poland on 17 September to stake out Soviet claims to the region. Warsaw fell on 27 September and Poland surrendered unconditionally to Germany.

Bad weather kept the action pretty much on hold for the next six months, while both sides prepared themselves for future actions. The Germans described this period of inactivity as the *Sitzkrieg;* the French as *la drôle de guerre*, the Phoney War. In April 1940, the war turned real.

Beginning on 9 April 1940, the Germans overran Denmark and part of Norway, then thundered into the neutral Low Countries of Luxembourg, Holland, and Belgium. Defenseless Luxembourg fell immediately, followed quickly by Holland on 14 May and Belgium on 26 May.

From 26 May through 4 June, the British and French evacuated some 340,000 troops from the French port of Dunkirk, one of the largest military evacuations ever. "Unfortunately," wrote British prime minister Winston Churchill, "several thousands remained who had gallantly protected the evacuation of their comrades."[8] Hitler then turned his back on the British and concentrated his attention on France.

British and French soldiers crowd into Dunkirk prior to being evacuated to Britain. Some 340,000 troops escaped the German onslaught.

14

On 5 June, the Germans attacked France en masse along the line of the Somme River. Five days later, after viewing Hitler's string of rapid successes, Italy declared war on Britain and France. The German juggernaut continued to roll, and France fell on 25 June.

Britain now stood alone to face the Nazi menace. In the summer of 1940, only the extraordinary heroics of Britain's Royal Air Force in the Battle of Britain (10 July–31 October) staved off a German invasion of England. Despite American aid engineered by President Franklin D. Roosevelt on a "cash and carry" basis, Britain was running critically short of weapons and war matériel and of the money to buy more. Britain's prospects began to look grim, but the British fought on.

An explosion at Pearl Harbor marks a direct hit on an American warship. The Japanese attack brought the United States into the war.

America Goes to War

On 22 June 1941, the war in Europe took a dramatic turn. The Germans amassed about 140 divisions along a one-thousand-mile front, from the Baltic to the Black Sea, and launched Operation Barbarossa—the invasion of Russia. Hitler caught the Soviets by complete surprise. "Hegemony [dominance] over Europe," he said, "will be decided in battle against *Russia*."[9] The Soviet Union suddenly found itself allied with Great Britain. Another ally would join them before the year was out.

On Sunday morning, 7 December 1941, Japan obviated any American isolationist concerns about whether or when the United States should enter World War II.

Striking without warning, Japanese carrier-based aircraft destroyed most of the U.S. Pacific Fleet at Pearl Harbor and demolished nearby U.S. military installations on the Hawaiian island of Oahu. President Roosevelt, speaking before Congress, called that day "a date which will live in infamy"[10] and asked Congress to declare war on Japan. Congress did.

On 11 December, Germany and Italy, who had signed a mutual defense agreement with Japan (1940 Tripartite Pact), took that as their cue to declare war on the United States. Thus, in the chaotic aftermath of Pearl Harbor, America went to war on two fronts—at a time when its armed forces were grossly unprepared to fight on even one.

Ike Takes Charge

Three days before Christmas 1941, Winston Churchill arrived in Washington for a series of meetings lasting into January 1942 known as the Arcadia Conference. Churchill and Roosevelt agreed to establish a unified Anglo-American general staff to coordinate Allied war plans against both Germany and Japan—a merging of the British Chiefs of Staff and the U.S. Joint Chiefs of Staff into the Combined Chiefs of Staff (CCS). Even as Japanese forces ran rampant in the Pacific and Far East—and before the first American troops became available for committing anywhere—the leaders further agreed to dedicate their combined energies and resources to first defeating Germany. Until then, they affirmed, the Allies would maintain a primarily defensive posture against Japan.

On 25 June 1942, Lieutenant General Dwight D. ("Ike") Eisenhower was appointed commander of U.S. forces in the European Theater, and American and British leaders entered into a series of strategy sessions to decide when and where to attack the Germans next. On 25 July, they decided on an invasion of French North Africa. They called it Operation Torch. The Allies designated Eisenhower as their commander.

A Trifling Delay

Operation Torch commenced on 8 November 1942 when American and British troops landed in Casablanca, Morocco, and in Algiers and Oran in Algeria. Their

In June 1942, Lieutenant General Dwight D. Eisenhower assumed command of all U.S. forces in the European Theater.

objectives were to seize Morocco, Algeria, and Tunisia as bases for future operations, linking the invasion forces with those of General Bernard Montgomery's British 8th Army to the east.

The Allied forces secured all of their objectives in three days, but they failed to follow up on their quick successes, and it cost them. Hitler immediately airlifted reinforcements into Tunisia and stopped the late-arriving Allied advance cold. What might have been a blitzkrieg-style Allied victory in North Africa bogged down in a wet-winter stalemate.

By March 1943, the Germans, now cut off from any hope of reinforcement or re-supply, were caught in a vise between two Allied armies. Field Marshal Erwin Rommel, perceiving the hopelessness of the German situation, noted, "A great gloom settled over us all. For the Army Group to remain longer in Africa was plain suicide."[11] On 9 March, Rommel turned over his command to General Jürgen von Arnim and left Africa for good going on extended sick leave.

Operation Torch and the Battle for North Africa lasted until 13 May 1943. The seemingly trifling two-week delay had set back the scheduled Normandy landings by a full year.

The Italian Campaigns

Following their victory in North Africa, the Allies spent the next two months preparing to invade and conquer Sicily, which was preliminary to invading Italy itself. Their objective, in the words of Winston Churchill, was to strike at "Axis-held Europe's soft underbelly along the Mediterranean."[12] Their further aim was to knock Italy out of the war.

The assault on Sicily, called Operation Husky, began on 10 July and lasted for

American troops roll into Palermo, the capital of Sicily, on 22 July 1943. The Sicilian campaign would end in victory for the Allies three weeks later.

thirty-eight days, ending with an Allied victory on 17 August. Italian dictator Benito Mussolini resigned on 25 July and was replaced by Marshal Pietro Badoglio. The capture of Sicily fully opened the Mediterranean sea routes to the Allies. Another important aspect of the Allied victory in Sicily was its effect on Hitler's decision to end all offensive operations on the Eastern Front so that reinforcements could be sent to Italy and the Balkans.

Allied equipment comes ashore at Salerno near a downed American plane. Stiff German resistance almost drove the Allies from the beachhead.

On the negative side, the Allies, despite mastery of the air and seas, could not prevent the evacuation of about 100,000 Axis troops across the Strait of Messina into Italy. They could follow them across the narrow waterway, however, which is what they did.

The Allies, hoping to exploit their quick success in Sicily, landed in strength at Salerno on the Italian mainland on 9 September 1943. The Italians had announced their surrender to the Allies a day earlier, but the Germans had rushed in replacements to fill their positions.

In the bitter fighting that followed, the Germans, under Field Marshal Albert Kesselring, nearly threw the Allied forces back into the sea. American lieutenant general Mark W. Clark later recalled that his officers were "stopping trucks, jeeps, and everything else that came along. Every soldier was given a gun and put in the line."[13] The Americans dug in and held

long enough for British general Sir Harold Alexander, overall commander of Allied forces in Italy, to rush in reinforcements to secure the beachhead.

Kesselring withdrew artfully, and the Allies thereafter broke out of the beachhead and drove on to capture the key Italian port of Naples on 1 October. The action, code-named Operation Avalanche, resulted in a narrow Allied victory but allowed Kesselring time to establish a strong defensive line along the Volturno River to the north. The Allies continued to advance, but slowly.

On the eastern front, a Soviet drive begun on 5 August established its first bridgehead across the Dnieper River on 22 September. Driving ever westward, the Soviets liberated Kiev on 7 November 1943.

Meanwhile, German defenses began collapsing along the Dnieper, the last German defensive line in Soviet territory.

Soviet leader Joseph Stalin kept pressure on the Allies to open a second front in the west, as he had almost since the day the Germans invaded Russia. Three weeks later, on 28 November 1943, Roosevelt, Churchill, and Stalin met in Tehran (Iran) to discuss plans for the invasion of Western Europe. On Christmas Eve, General Eisenhower was appointed supreme Allied commander for the impending invasion. In the meantime, the fighting intensified in Italy.

On 22 January 1944, the Allies landed at Anzio on the west coast of Italy, thirty miles south of Rome. Operation Shingle, as it was known, was designed to outflank the German Gustav Line and thus hasten the occupation of Cassino and the fall of Rome. As Winston Churchill was to write later, "I had hoped that we were hurling a wildcat onto the shore, but all we got was a stranded whale."[14]

Although heavy German resistance contained the Allied beachhead for four months of intensive fighting, the Allies eventually broke out of the perimeter in May and helped breach the Gustav Line and turn the battle for Cassino. As a result of bickering between Allied commanders, Kesselring's 10th Army escaped intact as a fighting force.

On 4 June 1944, on a moonlit night in Rome, a young Italian woman named Vera Signorelli Cacciatore watched the last of the Germans leave the city. "For half an

Life on the Beach

Life on the Anzio beachhead was grim for the American GI. In *The Mighty Endeavor*, Charles B. MacDonald, historian and former company commander in World War II, cites the view of an infantry replacement new to the beachhead.

It was just plain hell all through the day, and the nights were worse. The hole got about six inches of water, and you couldn't do anything except try to bail it out with your helmet. We wrapped shelter [pup tent] halves and blankets around us but they didn't do much good. They got soaked with rain and then you sat on a piece of wood or something and shivered and cussed. . . . You couldn't get out of that hole once the sun came up, or even show the top of your head. . . .

You had to get out of the hole when it got dark for several reasons, one of which was to get some circulation back into your feet. A lot of the boys went to the medics with bad cases of trench foot, but I wasn't that lucky.

Jerry [the Germans] threw in a lot of artillery and mortars. The best thing to do was pull in your head and pray. Some of that big stuff would cave in the side of a wet foxhole like it was sand, and a couple of the boys got buried right in their hole fifty yards away from me. We had two or three casualties every day, mostly from artillery and mortars. If you got it at night you were lucky, because they could get you out right away.

God help you if you got hit in the daytime.

The liberation of the European continent begins as American soldiers wade into battle at Normandy on 6 June 1944.

hour after the Germans' departure," she later recalled, "there was quiet and then someone yelled that the Americans are coming."[15] Rome belonged to General Mark Clark and the Americans, the first Axis capital to fall. The invasion of Normandy began a day and a half later.

After a four-month bombing campaign against rail and road targets in France, the largest amphibious landing in history commenced on 6 June 1944, a date renowned and commemorated the world over as D day. Since the planning in 1942, Operation Overlord, as the invasion was called, had been repeatedly delayed because of logistical difficulties and the sheer enormity of such an undertaking.

Airborne and glider-borne troops preceded the main assault forces on the night of 5–6 June, and were followed by amphibious landings early in the morning on five separate beaches. In less than a week, the Allies consolidated their beachheads and started to press inland. Field Marshal Erwin Rommel reported that his losses for the entire month of June would total "28 generals, 354 commanders and approximately 250,000 troops."[16] Although the fighting would continue for almost another year in Europe, the successful D day landings foretold the doom of Hitler's Nazi empire.

On 22 June 1944—the third anniversary of the German invasion of Russia—the Soviets, in step with the Allied invasion of Normandy, launched a massive summer offensive against the German Army Group Center. During the offensive, code-named Operation Bagration after a Russian general in the Napoleonic Wars, the Soviets advanced along a 350-mile front on the axis of Smolensk-Minsk-Warsaw. With air superiority and supported by a massive array of artillery (an estimated four hundred guns per mile of front), the Soviet armies annihilated thirty German divisions and moved three hundred miles closer to Germany. By the end of the year, the Soviets had reached the Baltic in the north and moved into the Balkans in the south.

By the winter of 1944, measured by almost any standard, Germany had long since lost the war—in the air, at sea, at Stalingrad and Kursk, on the beaches of Normandy, and in the Hürtgen Forest. The Germans had lost 3 million men in the fighting thus far, yet Hitler refused to quit. Instead, he launched an offensive.

The offensive was known by many as the Ardennes Offensive, but it was known to GIs as the Battle of the Bulge. Hitler called it *Wacht am Rhein* (Watch on the Rhine). It turned into the largest battle on the western front and the largest battle ever fought by the U.S. Army. Writes historian Stephen E. Ambrose,

Only a Handful Left

Before the Battle of the Bulge, there were several battles for the heavily wooded Hürtgen Forest, southeast of Aachen, Germany, and each was as senseless as it was bloody. In the following extract from Edward G. Miller's *A Dark and Bloody Ground*, Technical Sergeant George Morgan, USA, describes the action there.

The forest up there was a helluva eerie place to fight.... Show me a man who went through the battle . . . and who says he never had a feeling of fear, and I'll show you a liar. You can't get all of the dead because you can't find them, and they stay there to remind the guys advancing as to what might hit them. You can't get protection. You can't see. You can't get fields of fire. Artillery slashes the trees like a scythe. Everything is tangled. You can scarcely walk. Everybody is cold and wet, and the mixture of cold rain and sleet keeps falling. Then they jump off again, and soon there is only a handful of the old men left.

A soldier crouches in one of the few clearings of the Hürtgen Forest.

Of the 600,000 GIs involved, almost 20,000 were killed, another 20,000 were captured, and 40,000 were wounded. . . . Two U.S. infantry divisions were annihilated; in one of them, the 106th, 7,500 men surrendered, the largest mass surrender in the war against Germany.[17]

In the end, however, the American GIs prevailed with grit and superior armor and mobility. Hitler's last desperate gamble to snatch victory from almost certain defeat failed, but it delayed the Allied advance into the German heartland by about a month.

The Americans gained back seven days of their delayed advance at a bridge over the Rhine River at Remagen. To their great surprise, despite German efforts to destroy it, they found the Ludendorff Railway Bridge still standing on 7 March 1945. After some genuine heroics, the Americans secured the bridge and established a tiny bridgehead on the German side. Five divisions joined the bridgehead before the bridge collapsed ten days later. American GIs dubbed it a miracle. Because German troops had failed to knock down the bridge, German propaganda minister Joseph Goebbels called it "a raving scandal."[18]

The Allies followed up quickly in March, with further Rhine crossings at Boppard, Strasbourg, and between Bonn and Mainz. German defenses began collapsing, bringing the end of the war in Europe into view. It came on 8 May 1945.

Chapter 2

Operation Torch: The Battle for North Africa

"Munitions expended, weapons and war equipment destroyed. The Afrika Korps has fought to a standstill, as ordered."
—General Hans Cramer, last commander of the Afrika Korps,
in his last message to the German High Command
(quoted in the Editors of Time-Life Books, *WW II*)

When American GIs splashed ashore in French North Africa in late 1942, the U.S. Army began a ground campaign against the European Axis that was to continue almost without pause until Italy capitulated and Germany surrendered. Operation Torch, as the invasion was called, opened the tap on a flow of American troops into the Mediterranean Theater that would eventually pool into more than a million men.

Almost 4 million more would fight in Western Europe in the largest battle commitment ever undertaken by the U.S. Army. Along with their British, Canadian, French, and other allies, the GIs would reclaim most of Western Europe from under the heel of Nazi oppression, in a superb demonstration of coalition warfare.

The cooperative efforts of these combined forces would be augmented in Eastern Europe by the Soviets' massive contribution toward the ultimate Allied victory. It was partly because of Soviet leader Joseph Stalin's urgings for a second front in Western Europe that western coalition chiefs agreed to invade North Africa. But Stalin's continual pleas for a second front represented only one of many reasons the Allies chose to invade the area.

Politics Takes a Hand

Shortly after Pearl Harbor and America's entry into World War II, President Franklin Delano Roosevelt produced his first great leadership act: his decision to join Britain

President Franklin Delano Roosevelt signs the declaration of war against Germany.

As the war headed into 1942, the Americans joined their British allies in a series of protracted strategy debates about how best to defeat Hitler. Roosevelt's military advisers wanted to build up immediately for an invasion of the European mainland later in the year or early in 1943. Churchill and his counselors declared that an invasion of the Continent so soon would be next to impossible because of insufficient time to assemble the necessary forces and too few available landing craft in which to haul them across the English Channel. They also held reservations about the strength and inexperience of American armed forces and their ability to take on such a formidable task early on.

The British, who had long counted on America's entry into the war to turn impending defeat into victory, were shocked to discover the reality of their new ally's military unpreparedness. Sir John Dill, recent head of the Imperial General Staff, noted that Americans lacked "even the slightest conception of what war means, and their armed forces are more unready than it is possible to imagine."[20]

Churchill, and his cautious advisers, did not want to risk a failed invasion and the needless sacrifice of Allied men and matériel on European beaches. He insisted that a premature invasion represented "the

in putting the defeat of Germany in Europe ahead of that of Japan in the Pacific. Given the anger and vengeful mood of the American people toward Japan, it was a tough choice, but one that had to be made. He explained his decision simply: "Germany is the greater enemy; once we've defeated Germany, we shall be able to deal with Japan."[19]

only way in which we could possibly lose this war."[21] Churchill instead favored extending operations in North Africa, where British forces were already fighting. He cited several reasons.

Seizing French North Africa and beyond, he argued, would introduce American troops to the action, boost American morale, and appease Stalin's demands for a second front. This alternate plan, he contended, would yield "a springboard, not a sofa."[22] (Churchill envisaged follow-on offensive actions in Sicily and Italy rather than a lengthy period of inactivity that an enormous troop buildup for the invasion of Western Europe would entail.) But Roose-

velt's advisers were unreceptive to Churchill's plan and suggested redirecting U.S. efforts to the Pacific Theater.

In June 1942, Churchill, in the face of continuing disagreements, flatly told Roosevelt that Britain was both unable and unwilling to undertake the invasion of Europe in 1942 or even in 1943. Having already been driven from Norway, France, and Greece by the Germans, the British

Winston Churchill (with cigar) reviews a map with General Bernard Montgomery (pointing). Churchill did not wish to invade mainland Europe until American troops had experienced combat.

intended to stay the next time they landed on the Continent.

Roosevelt, over the dissenting voices of his reluctant advisers, accepted Churchill's proposal to invade French North Africa. He told his generals, "If we can't invade northern Europe, we must go somewhere else, and that somewhere else is not the Pacific." [23] Looking ahead to the congressional elections in the fall, the president wanted American troops in action against Hitler by then to help swing the vote in his party's favor.

On 25 August, Roosevelt directed that Operation Torch, the invasion of French North Africa, be launched on or before 30 October 1942. The date just happened to fall four days before the elections. Thus, politics took an early hand in how the United States fought the war.

Long Live France!

With the start of Operation Torch now set for just over two months away, the Allies had to scramble to map out their strategy and stage their invasion forces. When finalized, their war plan was split into three principal elements—the Western, Central, and Eastern Task Forces—and called for landings in Morocco and Algeria.

Torch's primary objective was to seize Tunisia before the Germans could occupy it from nearby Sicily. The Anglo-American invasion force in the west would then move east-

ward to link up with Lieutenant General Bernard L. Montgomery's British 8th Army, advancing westward through Libya. Together, the two Allied armies would form a vise within which to crush Field Marshal Erwin Rommel's 100,000-man German-Italian army in Libya, including his vaunted Afrika Korps. But first they had to deal with the French.

The Allies knew at the outset that moving against French North Africa would pose a political problem for them. It derived from the armistice that followed the fall of France in 1940. Under its terms, the Germans ceded control of much of southern France and France's colonial possessions to the Vichy France government, under French pro-German collaborator

At a staging area for Operation Torch, elements of the Allied invasion force prepare to board a transport.

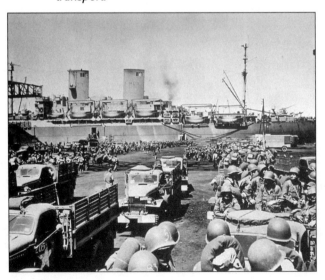

Marshal Philippe Pétain. Although a French resistance movement continued to fight the Germans inside France and a Free French Army was forming in the British Isles, the regular French Army and Navy left intact by the armistice were pledged to serve the Vichy regime.

The Allies hoped that the Vichy French defenders would not resist them in North Africa, but they could not be sure. Moreover, the British had already antagonized the French by attacking their fleet at Oran, Morocco, and elsewhere a year earlier. To avert unnecessary bloodshed, the Allies met secretly with trusted French leaders to enlist French sympathy in advance, but these efforts failed to produce any assurance that the French forces would not resist.

Partly due to the fractured Franco-British relations and partly because of the inability of the Allies to predict the French response, the Allies called on Lieutenant General Dwight D. Eisenhower to put aside his paperwork in Britain and command the operation. They designated British admiral Sir Andrew B. C. Cunningham to head naval operations. President Roosevelt, believing that the French would receive American assault troops more readily than British forces, insisted that the predominantly American landing forces be commanded by American generals.

Four days before the scheduled start of the landings, the Allies, particularly the British, received a great boost to their morale. General Montgomery's British 8th Army, in a curtain raiser for the Anglo-

The Uppermost Question

On 21 October 1942, the British submarine *Seraph* slipped its mooring at Gibraltar and charted course for French North Africa. The submarine carried Major General Mark Clark, a deputy of Lieutenant General Dwight D. Eisenhower. He was en route to a clandestine meeting with Robert Murphy, the U.S. consul general in North Africa, and representatives of the pro-German Vichy France government. (The Vichy France government was the regime authorized by the Germans on 2 July 1940 to govern unoccupied France and French colonial territories. It was based in Vichy, France, two hundred miles south of Paris. Vichy was also a city famous for its thermal springs, hence Vichy water.) The purpose of the meeting was to elicit from the French a pledge to aid—or at least not to resist—imminent Allied landings in French North Africa. Clark met with Murphy and the French agents the next day in a beach house, sixty miles west of Algiers. Beyond all else, Clark sought the answer to one question: Would the French fight?

Clark learned from the trusted French leaders that the French navy would likely offer more resistance than its army—if, in fact, either offered any resistance at all. There was a potential for real trouble at Casablanca, where the French superbattleship *Jean Bart* lay at anchor, along with a few cruisers and smaller warships. But General Clark returned to the *Seraph*—kayaking through heavy seas in which he lost his pants and almost drowned—with no assurance of French cooperation.

Two weeks later, when Anglo-American troops splashed ashore at three landing locales in French North Africa, one question loomed uppermost in the minds of most: Would the French fight?

American show in Morocco and Algeria, decisively defeated Field Marshal Rommel—the famed "Desert Fox"—and his Afrika Korps at El Alamein, Egypt.

On 4 November, England's King George VI wrote in his diary, "A victory at last . . . how good it is for the nerves."[24] The British victory saved the Suez Canal and sent Rommel's forces into a westward retreat across Libya.

Operation Torch got under way on 8 November 1942, ironically just after the November congressional elections in the United States. At 0300, seven hundred ships of the combined Anglo-American invasion fleet split into three smaller fleets and turned toward shore. At the same time, a familiar voice reached out to late-sitting radio listeners in northern Africa and southern Europe. In a prerecorded message transmitted across all broadcast bands, President Roosevelt, speaking resolutely in halting French, implored, "*Mes amis* (my friends). Have faith in our words. Help us where you are able." His short, direct message appealed to all loyal Frenchmen and freedom lovers to join with the liberators who were at that moment about to land on their shores. He closed with a flourish: "*Vive la France éternelle!*"[25] [Long live France!].

The Landings

Major General George S. Patton Jr., USA, commanded the Western Task Force— thirty-five thousand troops in thirty-nine vessels—which had been transported all the

Major General George S. Patton Jr. was in command of the Western Task Force. His objective was to land his troops at Casablanca.

way across the Atlantic from its staging area in the United States. A powerful naval squadron under Rear Admiral Henry K. Hewitt, USN, escorted Patton's landing force. Their main target was Casablanca, Morocco, on the Atlantic coast.

Major General Lloyd R. Fredendall, USA, headed the Central Task Force— thirty-nine thousand men in forty-seven ships—which arrived from Britain with a strong naval escort under Commodore Thomas H. Troubridge, RN. Their goal was Oran, Algeria, on the Mediterranean coast.

The Eastern Task Force—33,000 troops in thirty-four ships—led by Major General Charles W. Ryder, USA, also arrived from Britain, accompanied by a naval force under Vice Admiral Sir Harold M. Burroughs. Their mission was to capture Algiers, Algeria, also on the Mediterranean coast.

Before the landings at Casablanca, General Patton, who could curse like a pirate and write like a poet, issued a written proclamation to be read to the troops of his Western Task Force. It said, in part,

> The eyes of the world are watching us. The heart of America beats for us. God is with us. On our victory depends the freedom or slavery of the human race. We shall surely win.[26]

At 0515, Patton's Western Task Force commenced landings at Safi, 125 miles southwest of Casablanca; at Fedala, 15 miles northeast of it; and at Mehdia and Port Lyautey, 70 miles farther to the northeast. Vichy French troops, directed by French resident general August Noguès, resisted the American landings with violence and vigor, removing any doubt as to whether the French would fight.

In the Casablanca area, French warships challenged the U.S. fleet with a singular fury, but an overwhelming American response sank seven French warships and three submarines and inflicted about one thousand casualties on the defenders. Despite spirited French resistance, Patton's ground forces—the 3rd and 9th Infantry

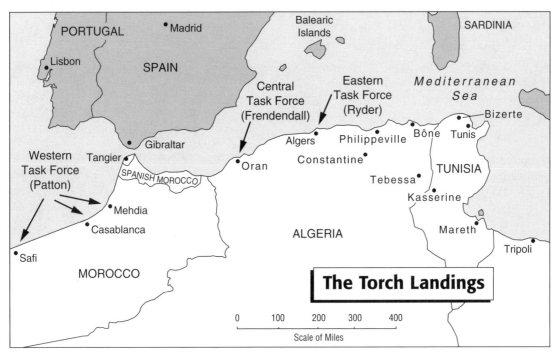

The Torch Landings

and 2nd Armored Divisions—gained their objectives and combined forces for a concentrated assault on Casablanca. The city capitulated on 11 November. An elated Patton afterward wrote,

> I said I would take Casa by D [day] plus 3 and I did. A nice birthday present [his 57th]. The God of fair beginnings has prospered here my hand. . . . To God be the praise.[27]

Meanwhile, at Oran, General Fredendall's Central Task Force also met stiff resistance on both sides of the city. But the U.S. 1st Infantry and 1st Armored Divisions persevered and presided over the city's surrender on 10 November.

At Algiers, the farthest Allied penetration into the Mediterranean, General Ryder's Eastern Task Force—a mix of British troops and regimental combat teams from the U.S. 1st Infantry and 1st Armored Divisions— enjoyed easier pickings. After only a brief show of force, French general Alphonse-Pierre Juin surrendered the capital city of Algeria on the evening of the invasion.

On 11 November, Admiral Jean Darlan, commander in chief of the Vichy forces, who happened to be visiting a sick son in Algiers, broke with Vichy and called for a general cease-fire.

The fighting in Algeria and Morocco cost the Allies 1,181 dead and missing plus 1,069 wounded; the French lost 1,600 dead and 1,000 wounded. Within four days, General Ike Eisenhower's forces had achieved their objectives.

Two days later, commenting on Allied successes in North Africa, Winston Churchill said, "There is a long road still to tread, but the end is sure."[28]

The Eastern Task Force encounters little opposition as it goes ashore near Algiers. The Algerian capital was captured on the evening of the invasion.

Politics Again

Several factors entered into the swift Allied victory, the first of which was surprise. Despite the size of their invasion fleet—at that time the largest ever assembled—it went undetected by the French until too late. The superior strength of Allied forces all but guaranteed the operation's successful outcome, but politics played an important role in keeping the casualties down on both sides.

On 15 November 1942, General Eisenhower and Admiral Cunningham drew up a formal accord with Admiral Darlan, installing the Frenchman as chief of a civil government in North Africa. Eisenhower took a lot of criticism over this so-called Darlan Deal. Because Darlan had collaborated with the Germans, many of the Allies felt that he could not be trusted, which was a fair assessment.

In fairness to Eisenhower, however, the accord ensured French cooperation, saved at least a few lives, solidified Allied bases in Morocco and Algeria, and expedited the start of subsequent operations. Even so, the British deplored the accord, and President Roosevelt, under growing criticism at home and from Britain, labeled it a "temporary expedient." [29]

On Christmas Eve 1942, a French student assassinated Darlan in Algiers. The Allies replaced him with French patriot General Henri-Honoré Giraud, thereby eliminating the source of discord. Winston Churchill later wrote, "Darlan's murder, however criminal, relieved the Allies of their embarrassment at working with him, and at the same time left them with all the advantages he had been able to bestow during the vital hours of the Allied landings." [30] Thus, once again, politics played a hand in Operation Torch.

Lost Opportunity

The Germans responded rapidly to Darlan's betrayal and the Allied landings in North Africa. Hitler immediately sent troops to occupy Vichy France and sent more troops and matériel into Tunisia to block an Allied eastward advance. He wanted to avoid becoming trapped in an Allied "nutcracker" at all costs since it would likely break his hold on North Africa.

Meanwhile, the time spent hammering out a political deal with Darlan, coupled with a shortage of trucks and other vehicles for transporting foot soldiers, had delayed the Allied drive into Tunisia. Serious contact with the Germans did not commence for almost two weeks. By then, the Germans had won the race for Tunisia.

Then weather conditions worsened, slowing Allied progress further yet. Colonel Karl Detzer, a roving editor who covered the entire operation for *Reader's Digest,* later described the scene:

The weather turned bad all along the front, and the brief season of winter rain brought mud to the hillsides of Tunisia and filled the wadis [streambeds] with brown and yellow water. Fog spread over the wet land and the nights turned cold. It was the mud that slowed our advance, held down the infantry, bogged the guns and for a time almost halted the trucks bringing up ammunition and food from the rear. It gave the Germans and Italians the time they desperately needed to prepare for a stand.[31]

Under cover of their Sicily-based aircraft, the Germans and Italians poured reinforcements into Tunisia, out of range of Allied aircraft operating out of Gibraltar. By month's end, seventeen thousand Axis troops, including the 10th Panzer Division, and one hundred tanks had been airlifted or shipped into Tunisia. And the Luftwaffe had become increasingly effective in harassing and impeding the Allied advance.

After the capture of Algiers, General Ryder turned over his Anglo-American troops to British lieutenant general Kenneth A. N. Anderson, as had been planned, and stepped aside. Anderson drove on Tunis over four hundred miles of narrow, clogged roads, with scant air cover and poor communications. His advance elements drew within fifteen miles of the city,

German tanks and support vehicles rush into Tunisia to reinforce Axis forces there. Hitler would stop at nothing to maintain his hold on North Africa.

Antiaircraft fire lights the nighttime skies over Algiers during a raid by the Luftwaffe.

but General Jürgen von Arnim's fresh Axis troops counterattacked with superior air support and forced him back.

By Christmas, Eisenhower, in a "bitter decision," conceded all hope of gaining control of Tunisia that winter. Any further offensive operations would have to wait until after the two-month rainy season. "It was now clear that the capture of Tunisia would be a prolonged struggle requiring a substantially revised strategy," wrote General Omar N. Bradley in his autobiography. "Moreover, the hope of trapping Rommel between Torch forces and Monty's Eighth Army had been irretrievably lost."[32]

Kasserine Pass

On 24 January 1943, British general Kenneth Anderson assumed command of the entire front. Two weeks later, General Eisenhower was named supreme commander of all Allied forces in Africa. General Sir Harold R. L. G. Alexander, commander of all British forces advancing from Libya, was named Ike's deputy and commander of ground forces, newly designated the 18th Army Group.

After a prolonged winter lull in the desert action, Rommel's German-Italian Panzer Army and Arnim's 5th Panzer Army launched a sudden attack in February 1943. The surprise offensive was aimed at preventing Eisenhower's Allied forces from reaching the Tunisian coast from the south and splitting the Axis ranks. In his flight from the British in Libya, Rommel had taken refuge behind the Mareth Line, an old French defensive line separating (French) Tunisia from (Italian) Libya. Here the panzer divisions were reequipped with the awesome fifty-six-ton Mark VI Tiger tanks, fitted with four inches of armor and armed with an eighty-eight-millimeter cannon and two heavy machine guns.

On 14 February, Valentine's Day, the 10th and 21st Panzer Divisions of Rommel's crack Afrika Korps lurched out of Faïd and churned toward Kasserine Pass, an obscure tuck in the desert landscape hedged in between steep, rocky cliffs. It did not even appear on Allied battle maps. Blocking their path to the threshold of the communications hub of Tébessa stood only the inexperienced and underequipped troops of General Lloyd Fredendall's 1st Armored Division and 168th Regimental Combat Team.

Kasserine Pass—or "Kerosene Pass," as the GIs called it—lay behind the American

GIs ride a captured Mark VI Tiger tank. Four inches of armor and an eighty-eight-millimeter cannon made the Tiger nearly invincible.

lines. The GIs faced a narrow gap between two steep mountains, designated Faïd Pass on their maps. The battle began on what had promised to be a quiet Sunday afternoon. There had been no sign of the enemy, nor was any expected. American tanks were scattered among several battalions, nowhere in sufficient strength to repulse a sustained attack by heavy armor. But that's what Rommel brought in plenty. Reports Colonel Detzer,

First the Stukas [dive-bombers] dived low, scooting down from the eastern hilltops, machine-gunning our infantry and bombing our artillery positions. Wave after wave, they poured out of the east in the heaviest aerial blow Americans had faced in Africa. Then out of the pass roared the German counterattack. The panzers were manned by Rommel's *Afrika Korps* veterans, and they smashed through the undermanned Allied forces and sent them reeling.

Our men fought bravely. But they had little air support, not enough guns of their own, not enough tanks concentrated anywhere to meet the furious assault. So they fell back to Kasserine. There they held for six days, dug into the hillside, with not enough food or water, not enough of anything except courage and the will to win.[33]

But they did not win. The Americans suffered their worst defeat in North Africa—a total rout. One American colonel in wild retreat reported that he was "just shifting positions," to which Colonel Thomas Drake snorted, "Shifting positions, hell! I know panic when I see it."[34]

Captain Allerton Cushman, an observer studying U.S. antitank weapons, offered a similar view of the rout:

As far as I could see were clouds of dust as vehicles raced away from the advancing enemy. I opened my camera. After all, I was an observer. But I couldn't bring myself to press the shutter. It was too awful a sight.[35]

Rommel's panzers drove back the green American GIs twenty-one miles in nine days. The Americans lost 192 dead and 2,624 wounded, plus another 2,459 captured and missing.

Just when it appeared that Rommel's panzers would break through the Allied lines, the GIs stiffened their defenses.

A Stuka releases its bombs. The Germans used dive-bombers to pummel the Americans at Kasserine Pass.

Aided by strong air support and the British 6th Armored Division counterattacking from the north, the Americans at last blunted Rommel's thrust. He began pulling back to his original positions on 22 February, in the end having taken losses equivalent to those of the Allies. Rommel's assault on Kasserine proved to be the last successful Axis offensive in North Africa.

"Mission Accomplished"

Two weeks later, General Eisenhower relieved General Lloyd R. Fredendall and placed General George S. Patton Jr. in command of the newly reconstituted U.S.

The GI

The abbreviation "GI" originally meant "galvanized iron" (as was used for garbage cans) and later was used to denote "government issue." Still later (circa 1943), it came to mean a member or former member of the armed forces of the United States, particularly the combat infantry soldier. Ernie Pyle, probably America's most-loved war correspondent of World War II, wrote of the combat infantryman in North Africa in 1943. (This extract appears in Peter G. Tsouras's *Warriors' Words*.)

> I love the infantrymen because they are the underdogs. They are the mud-rain-and-wind boys. They have no comforts, and they learn to live without the necessities. And in the end they are the guys that wars can't be won without.

Pyle's succinct tribute to the infantryman remains true to this day. Each succeeding generation of U.S. soldiers builds in turn on the proud heritage established by the American GI in World War II.

II Corps, made up of the 1st Armored and the 1st, 9th, and 34th Infantry Divisions. A ring of Allied steel began to close on the Axis forces.

On 9 March, Rommel, dispirited and exhausted, flew home. He could see the imminence of defeat and wanted to persuade Hitler to abandon Africa and thus save his troops from extinction. Hitler refused. Moreover, he forbade his ace commander to return to Tunisia. "Africa will be held," the Führer snapped, "and you must go on sick leave." [36] The irate Nazi dictator continued to pour troops and matériel into Tunisia, and General Arnim took over command of Rommel's forces, in addition to his own, under the umbrella of the newly formed Army Group Africa.

In mid-March, Patton's II Corps, quickly galvanized into an effective fighting force by their twin ivory-handled, silver-pistol-toting commander, took the offensive. The night before the start of what history calls the Battle of El Guettar, Patton gravely told his staff, "Gentlemen, tomorrow we attack. If we are not victorious, let no one come back alive." [37] His II Corps took on a panzer division and decisively defeated it. New Sherman tanks with high-velocity seventy-five-millimeter guns proved a match for German Panzer IV medium tanks and contributed greatly to the GI victory. The process of redemption for Kasserine had begun.

On 26 March, Montgomery's British 8th Army breached the Mareth Line, and it drove through German defenses at Gabès on 6 April. The next day, a patrol from the

U.S. 9th Division met a patrol from Montgomery's 4th Indian Division, linking all of Alexander's ground forces. Thereafter, the Anglo-American pincers closed hard and fast on the cities of Tunis and Bizerte.

On 7 May 1943, the two cities fell simultaneously. The Allied conquerors captured 250,000 prisoners, most of them German, including General Arnim. During the six-month Tunisian campaign, Axis dead and wounded numbered about 40,000. American casualties totaled 18,500, including 2,184 killed. The British suffered 33,000 casualties.

Axis prisoners are marched out of Tunis after the city's fall to the Allies. At the end of Operation Torch, one-quarter of a million men surrendered to British and American forces.

The Allies now owned all of North Africa, and the European Axis forces were finally forced on the defensive. They would remain there for the rest of the war. In addition, the victory in North Africa helped clear the Mediterranean sea-lanes for Allied use. As added pluses of Operation Torch, American GIs had emerged from their baptism of fire as effective combat soldiers, General Eisenhower had gained invaluable command experience, and the Allies had learned to function efficiently as coalition forces.

On 9 May, two days after the fall of Tunis and Bizerte, General Omar Bradley (who had taken over command of II Corps so that Patton could prepare the U.S. 7th Army for the next Mediterranean operation) took great delight in cabling a two-word message to Eisenhower: "Mission Accomplished." [38]

In only two months, another mission would commence on the Italian island of Sicily. It lay across a slim swath of the Mediterranean from Tunisia—only a "springboard's" leap away.

Chapter 3

Operation Husky: The Battle for Sicily

> *"This is a horse race in which the prestige of the U.S. Army is at stake. We must take Messina before the British."*
>
> —Major General George S. Patton Jr., USA
> (quoted in Editors of Time-Life Books, *WW II*)

After their workmanlike victory in North Africa, the Allies turned their attention to the big Italian island of Sicily. Had they planned to launch their invasion under the worst weather conditions imaginable, they probably could not have improved on the high winds and heaving seas occasioned by nature on 9 July 1943, the day before D day at Sicily. Two airborne assaults spearheading the main landing forces paid the price for nature's fury.

Commencing shortly after midnight on the night of 9–10 July, following a month-long air and naval bombardment of Axis air bases in Sicily, Sardinia, and Italy, fifteen hundred glider-borne troops from the British 1st Airborne Division took to the air to seize a vital bridge behind the designated British invasion beaches. At the same time, thirty-four hundred paratroopers of the newly created U.S. 82nd Airborne Division—the first American unit of its kind—set off for Gela to secure the roads and high ground behind the American landing beaches. Because of gale-force winds, a complex flight plan, and pilot inexperience, both advance assaults met with near disaster.

Both airborne elements, 4,900 troops in all, left from Tunisia ferried by 366 aircraft—331 C-47 transports to drop the U.S. paratroopers plus 35 Albemarle reconnaissance-bombers to tow the British troops. The Allied pilots lacked combat experience and were new to airborne, over-water, and night

American soldiers inspect the wreckage of a British glider in Sicily. More than 90 percent of the gliders were lost at sea or missed their objectives.

operations against enemy installations. High winds of 33 miles per hour or more blew their aircraft off course. Some planes became lost and returned to base or were never seen again. Some pilots released their gliders too soon, and they were lost at sea. Only 54 of 144 British gliders landed in Sicily; of those, only 12—with about 100 men—touched down near their objective. The Americans fared little better and ended up scattered across a thousand-square-mile area of Sicilian countryside—few landed anywhere near their objective, many in the British drop zone. General of the Army Omar N. Bradley noted later,

> For a long time, [Colonel James M.] Gavin and the others [the reinforced 505th Parachute Regimental Combat Team] were not even certain they

were in Sicily. It was not an auspicious beginning; we would soon feel the loss of the paratroopers.[39]

Never before had the Allies attempted an airborne operation of such magnitude. Early results of this one did not augur well for its success—or for that of the Allied invasion of Sicily.

Of Mules and Men

Long before the outcome of Operation Torch had been decided, President Roosevelt and Prime Minister Churchill and their aides met at the Casablanca Conference (14–23 January 1943) to draft plans for the invasion of Sicily. They called it Operation Husky. The Sicily invasion would kick off the campaign for Italy in July 1943 and would last until May 1945.

Once the Allies had decided to invade North Africa at the Arcadia Conference in Washington, the subsequent move against Sicily (and later mainland Italy) became little more than a foregone conclusion. It would have been impractical, if not unfeasible, to move several hundred thousand troops and enormous matériel tonnage to Britain only to remain idle or stockpiled while awaiting the invasion of Normandy, almost a year distant. Also, it behooved the Allies to protect their interests in the Mediterranean Theater by keeping the pressure on the European Axis. The capture of Sicily would not only open the entire Mediterranean for Allied shipping, but it would continue to divert German troops from the Eastern Front, which would relieve the hard-pressed Soviets. (For example, Hitler ordered an end to the fighting at Kursk—the largest tank battle of the war—when the Allies landed in Sicily because of their imminent threat to Italy. Kursk marked the end of German offensives in Russia and the start of the first Soviet summer offensive of the war.)

The Combined Chiefs of Staff (CCS) again named General Eisenhower Allied supreme commander, with British chief subordinates: General Sir Harold Alexander, commander of the 15th Army Group (160,000 troops); Air Chief Marshal Sir Edward Tedder; and Admiral of the Fleet Andrew Cunningham. The CCS set 10 July 1943 for the invasion of Sicily.

Sicily, the largest island in the Mediterranean Sea, lies just off the toe of the Italian boot, separated by the narrow, two-mile-wide Strait of Messina. The Allied battle plan called for General Bernard Montgomery's British 8th Army to land on the southeast corner of the island. It was to drive up the east coast to Messina to cut off any enemy attempt to evacuate the island. General George Patton's 7th Army drew—much to Patton's displeasure—the more pedestrian assignment of guarding Montgomery's left flank and rear.

On Sicily, a 405,000-man Axis force—315,000 Italians and 90,000 Germans—under Italian general Alfredo Guzzoni awaited the Allies. It comprised six Italian coastal divisions (made up of mostly Italian reservists), four regular Italian divisions, and two fine German divisions—the 15th Panzer Grenadier (mechanized) Division and the Hermann Göring Panzer Division. Because of earlier encounters with the Italians and their tendency to surrender readily, the Allies expected only mild resistance from them. Commented journalist Romano Giachetti,

It was a curious position. Men still armed were forced to fire at an enemy that was actually their friend. The enemy was among them: Fascists and Germans.[40]

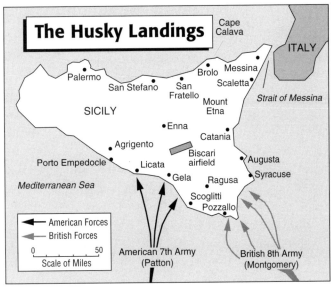

Italian soldiers were fast wearying of Mussolini's war, most recently demonstrated on 11 June 1943 on Pantelleria, an island stepping-stone between Tunisia and Sicily. An eleven-thousand-man Italian garrison had surrendered the island before a British invasion fleet could land a man. The only casualty of the operation came when a mule bit a British soldier.

Escape from Hell

After the initial abortive airborne operations, the seaborne landings along Sicily's eastern and southern shores enjoyed far greater success. (American paratroopers suffered 27 percent casualties; British glider-borne troops 23 percent. The casualties resulted mostly from running afoul of mistral winds—a form of unpredictable gale common to the Mediterranean—but also partly from "friendly" antiaircraft fire. Two nights after the landings, U.S. naval gunfire mistakenly knocked down several American aircraft.) The ship-to-shore activities got under way at 0245 on the morning of 10 July.

The Sicily landings showcased the latest products of Anglo-American marine architecture and ingenuity. The very latest in landing craft and amphibians were unveiled here: the 1,500-ton, 328-foot landing ship, tank (LST); the 550-ton, 112-foot landing craft, tank (LCT); and the 200-ton, 158-foot landing craft, infantry (LCI). The LST—dubbed "large stationary target" by the GIs—performed workhorse invasion

American tanks disembark from an LST in Sicily. LSTs and other landing craft made their debut during Operation Husky.

chores. It ran up on the beaches, opened wide its bow doors, lowered a ramp on cables, and spewed out troops, tanks, sundry kinds of vehicles, and all manner of supplies for the well-equipped modern soldier. The LST could also discharge other kinds of landing craft offshore, one of which was the amphibious DUKW, or "Duck." A six-wheeled boat-shaped truck, the DUKW was a GI favorite named for its factory designation (D = model year, U = amphibian, K = all-wheel drive, W = dual rear axles).

The Sicilian invasion fleet of some three thousand ships and landing craft was the largest amphibious force ever assembled to date—larger on the first day than the later Normandy armada. Because of the nearness of Tunisian ports, many of the smaller craft sailed directly from North Africa, making Sicily also a shore-to-shore operation. Riding out the swells of the mistral-wracked seas in the plunging, wallowing assault craft and breathing the nauseating fumes of inboard diesel engines, made for something short of a pleasure cruise, as Ernie Pyle described it:

> The little subchasers and infantry-carrying assault craft would disappear completely into the wave-troughs as we watched them. The next moment they would be carried so high they seemed to leap clear out of the water. . . . During the worst of the blow we hoped and prayed that the weather would moderate by dusk [of 9 July]. It didn't. . . . Never in my life had I been so depressed.[41]

When the first wave of landing craft scudded ashore, it is likely that few among the sallow-faced Allied troops would not have gladly stormed the gates of hell itself to escape the worse hell of seasickness. As naval historian Samuel Eliot Morison so aptly put it, "No power on earth could prevent them from establishing their beachheads."[42]

The Beachheads

As something good can often be found in even the worst of situations, the mistral winds served one useful purpose from an Allied perspective: The brutal weather helped the Allies achieve a modicum of surprise. Although not unaware of an imminent Allied invasion, the Axis forces hardly expected it to come in the wake of a wild mistral blow. When dawn broke on D day, the winds had let up, the seas had subsided, and a wall of Allied ships ringed a good third of the Sicilian coastline. Sicilians later described the scene to Samuel Eliot Morison:

No Way of Knowing

In the following extract from John Steinbeck's "Fear of Death as Green Troops Sail to Invasion," an article written for the New York *Herald Tribune* (and reprinted in Library of America's *Reporting World War II*), Steinbeck describes green American troops on the eve of the Sicily invasion.

> These are green troops. They have been trained to a fine point, hardened and instructed, and they lack only one thing to make them soldiers, enemy fire, and they will never be soldiers until they have it. No one, least of all themselves, knows what they will do when the terrible thing happens. No man there knows whether he can take it, knows whether he will run away or stick, or lose his nerve and go to pieces, or will be a good soldier. There is no way of knowing and probably that one thing bothers you more than anything else.
>
> And that is the difference between green troops and soldiers. Tomorrow at this time these men, those who are living, will be different. They will know then what they can't know tonight. They will know how they face fire.

There were thousands of vessels in the roadstead; one couldn't see the horizon for the ships. Thousands of troops were landing every minute.[43]

It was an exaggeration, as Morison notes, but nonetheless an awe-inspiring sight. Despite the predawn misfortunes, the first landings, covered by supporting naval gunfire, went well.

Three infantry divisions of Patton's 7th Army—the 3d, 1st, and 45th—poured ashore at Licata, Gela, and Scoglitti, respectively. Except at Gela, where Axis artillery harassed the "Big Red One" division all day and Italian and German counterattacks briefly threatened to shove it back into the sea, the Americans established beachheads quickly and with few problems.

Offshore, a German Stuka dive-bomber roared in over the invasion fleet at first light. It scored a hit on the stern of the U.S. destroyer *Maddox*, sending the destroyer—and most of its crew—to the bottom within minutes. Another German bomber sank a minesweeper moments later. A second U.S. destroyer extracted a measure of revenge from the Germans later that morning. When the Hermann Göring Panzer Division attacked the 1st Division beachhead with just over one hundred tanks—including seventeen new Mark VI Tigers—the *Cowie* (DD 632) zeroed in on the tanks with its five-inch guns. The destroyer's guns repulsed the tanks, and the *Cowie* won the first ever destroyer-tank battle. Despite a second German tank attack later that morning,

barely fended off by the 45th Division, General Eisenhower was still able to report before noon, "The success of the landings is already assured."[44]

Farther to the east along the one-hundred-mile coastal front, Montgomery's British 8th Army landed at points covering the southeast corner of the island, from near Pozzallo on the southwest shore to Avola on the eastern shore. The 8th Army comprised the 30th Corps in the west and the 13th Corps in the east. Both corps encountered only scattered opposition.

By the end of the first day, all of the beachheads had been carved out ashore, and the buildup of some fourteen thousand vehicles, six hundred tanks, eighteen hundred artillery pieces, and huge stacks of provisions was well under way. General Omar Bradley wrote later, "All our forces had got ashore with negligible casualties and were displaying remarkable aggressiveness."[45]

Holding On at Gela

Although the crisis at the Gela beachhead had been averted temporarily, General Patton decided to send the 2nd Armored Division—his floating reserve—ashore that night. He expected the enemy forces to return the next day in strength and wanted to be prepared. True to his expectations, the panzers showed some aggressiveness of their own the next day, 11 July, with an even stronger attack on the beachhead east of Gela. General Bradley later recalled,

That day, for many hours, the issue was in grave doubt. The German tanks crunched down to within a mile of the beaches. On every hand heroism was commonplace. Jim Gavin [airborne commander] approached to within ten feet of a Tiger tank and fired at it point-blank with our newest portable anti-tank weapon, the bazooka. The shell—far too small—simply bounced harmlessly off the tank. Bill Darby [ranger commander] turned some captured Italian guns against the tanks and blazed away. But none of this heroism was sufficient.[46]

Again, the U.S. Navy's big guns came to the aid of the besieged GIs. The U.S. cruisers *Boise* and *Savannah* and a flock of destroyers pummeled the tanks with repeated, well-directed five- and eight-inch salvos and turned them back. The two-day battle cost the Hermann Göring Panzer Division half its committed armor—fifty-five tanks, including ten awesome Tigers. By the end of their second day ashore, the GIs had secured the beachhead at Gela and held the once-doubtful issue well in hand.

In support of GIs at the Gela beachhead, a U.S. cruiser fires its guns against the tanks of the Hermann Göring Panzer division.

The End Results

East of Gela, the U.S. 45th Infantry Division captured the airfield at Biscari (Acate) and linked up with the Canadian 1st Division at Ragusa. Loss of the airfield cost the enemy eighty planes and control of the Sicilian skies. It also cost General Patton an untoward blemish on his record and began a deterioration in his relationship with General Bradley.

The realities of war's savagery cannot be exhibited more clearly than in the following account of two incidents that occurred near the Biscari airfield on 14 July. Reports British historian Martin Gilbert,

After twelve American infantrymen [of the 45th Infantry Division] had been wounded by sniper fire, a group of thirty-six Italians . . . surrendered. On the order of the American company commander they were lined up along the edge of a nearby ravine and shot. That same day, another American infantry company ordered forty-five Italian and three German prisoners of war to be sent back to the rear for interrogation. After they had gone about a mile, the sergeant of the escort ordered them to halt, declared that he was going to kill the "sons of bitches," borrowed a sub-machine gun, and shot the prisoners down.[47]

When General Bradley heard of the shootings and reported them to General Patton, Patton directed him "to tell the officer responsible for the shootings to certify that the dead men were snipers or had attempted to escape or something, as it would make a stink in the press and would also make the civilians mad. Anyhow, they are dead, so nothing can be done about it."[48] Bradley refused.

The two men were subsequently court-martialed, and the sergeant was found guilty and sentenced to life imprisonment. The company commander was found not guilty. A protracted protest of unfair discrimination between officers and enlisted

General Omar Bradley refused to obey an order that would have justified the murder of German and Italian prisoners of war near the Biscari airfield.

men resulted in the sergeant's release and return to active duty after serving only a year. By then, the company commander had been killed in action.

In fairness to Patton, the notes of Chester Hansen (Bradley's aide and collaborator in his World War II memoir *A Soldier's Story*) indicate that, when informed by Bradley of the affair, Patton snapped, "Try the bastards!"[49] Neither response alters the end results.

Patton Takes Palermo

Meanwhile, in the east, Montgomery's 8th Army drove rapidly to the north against weak resistance, capturing the port of Syracuse on 12 July and Augusta two days later. Advancing on two axes, the British 13th Corps continued north toward Catania, while the 30th Corps pushed on toward a network of roads near Enna and Leonforte.

On 15 July, Patton regrouped his forces. He formed a provisional brigade (a temporary unit formed for a specific task) under his deputy Lieutenant General Geoffrey Keyes, intending to seize Palermo in the northwest—and a claim to personal glory along with it. The new brigade consisted of the 2nd Armored, 3rd Infantry, and 82nd Airborne Divisions. At the same time, Patton intended to send Bradley's II Corps, made up of the 1st and 45th Divisions, thrusting up the center of the island to isolate Axis forces in the western half of the island. But 15th Army Group commander Alexander ordered Patton to continue

shielding the British 8th Army's left flank. This deprived Bradley's II Corps of the opportunity to cut the island in half quickly and snare the 15th Panzer Grenadiers escaping to the east.

Patton, however, with a covetous eye on Palermo—the island's capital—and unwilling to accept a subordinate role, flew to Tunisia to confer with Alexander. Confronting Alexander, Patton said, "General, I am here to ask you to take the wraps off me and change your orders to read, 'The Seventh Army will drive rapidly to the northwest and north and capture Palermo.'"[50] Alexander, surprised by Patton's audacity and conviction, consented.

With the "wraps off," Patton sent Keyes's provisional brigade dashing north and northwest in a whirlwind advance that covered a hundred miles in four days and cleared the western half of the island. The brigade met only token resistance, but sizzling summer heat and choking dust billowing off gravel roads dogged the GIs every step of the way. They entered Palermo on 22 July to find the Germans gone and throngs of Italians waiting to surrender. General Bradley, with undisguised sarcasm, later wrote,

> Patton's 100-mile dash to Palermo against spotty opposition was great theater and it generated the headlines he so craved. . . .
>
> However meaningless in a strategic sense, it was our most dramatic and

crowed-about "success" to date. It made our soldiers proud, lifted spirits at home, and impressed Alexander.[51]

It also delivered a major port into Allied hands, cleared the western half of the island, and displayed to the world the lightning mobility of U.S. forces under the competent leadership of Patton and his superbly capable subordinate commanders. The dash to Palermo cost the Americans 57 dead, 170 wounded, and 45 missing, against 2,900 enemy killed and 53,000 taken captive.

Italian troops surrender at Palermo. The drive on the capital met with little resistance and demonstrated the lightning mobility of Patton's forces.

Slaps Heard Round the World

On the same day that Patton liberated Palermo, Bradley's II Corps smashed through the center of Sicily to San Stefano on the north coast. By then, however, the delay in cutting off the eastward flight of the Germans had given them time to establish three defensive lines in front of Mount Etna, a 10,902-foot-high active volcano near the eastern coast. The German defense perimeter began at Catania on the east coast and slanted diagonally northward to San Stefano.

Sicily's rugged landscape restricted armored movement to a network of narrow, winding roads, much to the advantage of the German defenders. The Germans— now led by Colonel General Hans Hube, a canny, one-armed veteran of the eastern front—knew that the battle for Sicily had already been lost, but they were determined to resist as long as possible. Allied troops that were kept busy in Sicily, they reasoned, could not pose a threat anywhere else. Montgomery's 8th Army ran up against Hube's defenders on the Catania plains, south of Mount Etna, and temporarily bogged down.

In the west, Patton received orders from Eisenhower to march on Messina. Patton's 7th Army had now achieved equal status with Montgomery's 8th, and "Old Blood and Guts," as the press now called Patton, meant to make the most of it. Bradley's II Corps turned to the east and spearheaded the 7th Army thrust with two drives toward Messina. Major General Troy H. Middleton's 45th Division advanced along the coast road (Route 113), and Major General Terry de la Mesa Allen's Big Red

One wheeled along the parallel Nicosia-Randazzo highway (Route 120) twenty miles inland. This diverted pressure from Montgomery's troops, enabling them to take Catania on 5 August. After a fierce seven-day battle, Bradley's 1st Division and two regiments from the 9th Division (newly landed at Palermo) took Troina, due west of Mount Etna, when the Germans fell back to another line.

It was near Troina that Patton, while visiting wounded GIs at an evacuation hospital, committed the first of two acts that would forever sully his personal and professional reputation. At the hospital, Patton encountered a private who appeared uninjured and Patton asked him what was wrong with him. The private replied that he was not wounded and added, "I guess I can't take it."[52] (Doctors had diagnosed him as suffering from a moderately severe

Two columns of vehicles negotiate a mountain pass in Sicily. The island's rugged terrain limited the movement of U.S. troops and armor.

anxiety state of psychoneurosis, a condition for which he had been evacuated twice before.)

Patton exploded. He cursed the private, slapped him across the face with his gloves, called him a coward and a disgrace, and then seized him by the collar and threw him out of the hospital tent. That night, Patton noted in his journal that he had met

> the only arrant [shameless] coward I have ever seen in this army. . . . Companies should deal with such men, and if they [such men] shirk their duties, they should be tried for cowardice and shot.[53]

Later, it developed that the private had been suffering from chronic diarrhea and malaria and had a fever of 102.2 degrees. Patton did not know it at the time and apparently acted out of his concern that any form of cowardice worked insidiously to erode the character of a fighting unit. This event went unnoticed for a time, but a second incident soon followed.

On 10 August, while visiting a second field hospital, Patton encountered another soldier who had no apparent wounds but was diagnosed with severe shell shock (now called post-traumatic stress disorder or PTSD). "It's my nerves,"[54] the soldier said.

Patton visits with GIs wounded in battle. The general stained his reputation by slapping two soldiers whom he accused of being cowards under fire.

"Your nerves, hell! You are just a god-damned coward, you yellow son of a bitch!" Patton drew one of his ivory-handled pistols. "You ought to be shot. In fact I ought to shoot you right now, goddamn you!"[55] The soldier started weeping, and Patton slapped his face. At that point the doctor in charge of the hospital stepped between the general and the soldier and persuaded Patton to leave the tent.

When word of the slapping incidents reached Eisenhower, only his high regard for Patton's combat generalship kept him from relieving Patton on the spot. Instead, Ike ordered Patton to make a public apology to all concerned. Patton did and thereby saved his brilliant fighting career, however tarnished. Eisenhower then dismissed the matter, but before the news media finished covering the slapping incidents, the slaps administered by Patton could be heard round the world.

Coming of Age

Still smarting from Eisenhower's rebuke and the harsh press coverage of his actions, Patton pushed his forces on toward Messina, through their last fierce engagements between San Fratello and Sant' Agata. Simultaneously, Montgomery's troops hammered their way northeastward on either side of Mount Etna. Patton won the "horse race" to Messina, arriving there at 1000 on 17 August—only an hour ahead of a British column.

Upon arriving, the British commander climbed down off his tank, shook hands with Patton, and said, "It was a jolly good race. I congratulate you."[56] To the winner goes the wreath, which in Patton's case came in the form of a Distinguished Service Cross (his second), awarded to him by Ike for personal bravery.

Afterward, in a reflective mood, Patton said, "If I had to fight the campaign over, I would make no change in anything I did. Few generals in history have ever been able to say as much." But he was quick to share his triumph in a moving order of the day:

> I am really proud of the 7th Army. . . . I feel very humble it was the superior fighting ability of the American soldier, the wonderful efficiency of our mechanical transport, the work of Bradley, Keyes and the Army staff that did the trick. I just came along for the ride. . . . I certainly love war.[57]

Notwithstanding Patton's personal triumph and pride in his unit, the Sicily campaign fell short of perfection.

Despite the Allies' air and naval superiority, the Axis forces conducted a well-planned and well-executed evacuation of troops and matériel across the narrow Strait of Messina. In only six days and seven nights, the Germans evacuated almost 40,000 troops, 47 tanks, 94 heavy guns, more than 2,000 tons of ammunition, and many more tons of equipment; the Italians evacuated 62,000 troops, 41 big guns, and 12 mules. The lack of a coordinated Allied plan to cut off the evacuation made the exodus possible. Hitler had adamantly opposed the withdrawal at first, but when Mussolini was forced to resign on 25 July, Hitler lent his approval.

Axis casualties totaled more than 164,000, including 32,000 Germans. American casualties numbered 7,319; British losses were 9,353.

On the plus side of the Allied battle ledger, the Allies achieved their objectives in thirty-eight days, conquering Sicily, effecting the collapse of Mussolini's fascist regime and Italy's surrender (8 September 1943), and gaining absolute control over the Mediterranean Sea. Also, the Allies introduced new air, sea, and ground equipment; battlefield commanders gained valuable experience in airborne and amphibious operations; and—not least—the American GI came of age as a fighting man. He now stood equal to the tasks that awaited him on the Italian mainland.

Chapter 4

Salerno-Anzio-Rapido: The Italian Campaign

"I never again expect to witness such scenes of sheer joy. We would dock in Naples harbor unopposed, with an olive branch in one hand and an opera ticket in the other."
—Major Warren A. Thrasher, USA, on the reaction of shipboard, Salerno-bound GIs to the announcement of Italy's surrender on 8 September 1943 (quoted in Charles B. MacDonald, *The Mighty Endeavor*)

American GIs and their counterpart British Tommies found little on the beaches of Salerno to warrant their jubilance over the news of Italy's capitulation. Instead of peace symbols they carried instruments of death; rather than arias they heard the shrieks of the wounded and the moans of the dying. The Italians had surrendered; the Germans had not.

Although Italian marshal Pietro Badoglio, Mussolini's successor, officially professed his intentions of continuing hostilities, he had secretly opened negotiations with the Allies through agents in Lisbon in August 1943. Hitler, unaware of the Italian peace-feeler but suspicious of Badoglio's intentions, ordered German reinforcements into Italy. He increased his forces in Italy from six divisions in July to eighteen in September, with four more on their way. When the Allies announced the Italian armistice on 8 September 1943, the Italians laid down their arms and the Germans inherited most of Italy by default. When American GIs and British Tommies hit the beaches the next day, they found the Germans ready and waiting for them.

Operation Avalanche

The Allies had reached a final decision to invade Italy on 26 July 1943. On the same day, the Combined Chiefs of Staff sent this message to General Dwight D. Eisenhower: "You should plan forthwith landings in the Bay of Salerno, to be mounted at the earliest possible date, using the resources already available to you."[58] Eisenhower set 9 September 1943 as the "earliest possible date" for the Salerno landings, now termed *Operation Avalanche*. General Sir Harold Alexander's 15th Army Group would again provide the "resources."

Alexander's group now comprised two armies, the British 8th Army, under General Bernard L. Montgomery, and the Anglo-American 5th Army, under Lieutenant General Mark W. Clark. The 8th Army was to land at Reggio Calabria, in the

The Bay of Salerno was the objective of Operation Avalanche. The Allies chose to land there because it provided access to the port city of Naples.

toe of the Italian boot. When it had drawn the German defenders southward, the 5th Army would land behind them at Salerno and cut them off.

Salerno was chosen because it lay just within the range of covering Allied aircraft based in Sicily. (Carrier-based aircraft were unavailable because most Allied aircraft carriers had been sent to the Pacific.) Also, a successful landing would provide access to the key port city of Naples, twenty-nine miles to the northwest, which the Allies hoped to use as a base for supplying future operations.

On 3 September—the same day that the Allied-Italian armistice had been signed in secret—Montgomery's British 8th Army crossed the Strait of Messina into Calabria. But the Germans, under Field Marshal Albert Kesselring, field commander of all German forces in Italy, had anticipated an Allied crossover from Sicily and were already withdrawing to the north. The British, in keeping with their leader's style, commenced a slow, cautious advance up the boot, and the struggle for the Italian peninsula began. It would last until May 1945.

On the evening of 8 September, after General Eisenhower announced the formal surrender of the Italian government, the main elements of the Italian fleet sailed for

British-held Malta. The British 1st Airborne and 78th Divisions occupied the Italian naval base at Taranto, in the heel of the boot, on the 9th. At 0400 that same day, following a heavy preliminary bombardment, Clark's 5th Army, in concert with covering aircraft and supporting naval gunfire, started landing at Salerno.

The U.S. VI Corps, commanded by Major General Ernest J. Dawley (later relieved by Major General John P. Lucas), hit the southern beaches to protect the Allied right flank and link up with Montgomery's 8th Army, moving up from the south. The first wave landed safely, but as the second wave neared the shore in the predawn darkness, an amplified, German-accented voice boomed out in English over a loudspeaker: "Come on in and give up. You're covered!"[59] Then the eerie white light of flares lit up the sky and exposed them to

the raking fire of German guns positioned above the beachhead. They *were* indeed covered. But they still went in and staked out a chunk of sand and gradually established a foothold.

In the next three days, the U.S. 36th and 45th Infantry Divisions captured the ancient city of Paestum (founded in the 6th century B.C. by Greek colonists) and drove ten miles inland. On their left, Lieutenant General Sir Richard L. McCreery's British X Corps (46th and 56th Divisions) secured Battipaglia, near the center of the beachhead, and the town of Salerno, along the northern flank.

The realities of war quickly affected American GIs in their first exposure to

A British vessel escorts an Italian submarine to Malta. The main units of the Italian fleet surrendered to the Allies on 8 September.

As an Italian soldier looks on, American troops display a flag they captured near the city of Paestum.

combat. Harry Gunlock, of the 36th Infantry Division, recalled the distinct change in outlook that he and his uniniti-ated comrades experienced at Salerno:

> I remember when we went ashore we were gung-ho. At last we were in action and our blood was flowing fast. We wanted to get with it, but as the day wore on, and we saw the toll being taken, and the carnage, the idea of survival became our #1 priority.[60]

The situation turned critical on 12 September when the Germans, supported by the Luftwaffe and heavy armor, launched a powerful counterattack, recapturing Battipaglia and driving to within two miles of the sea. Offshore, German glider bombs scored direct hits on the American cruisers *Philadelphia* and *Savannah* and the British battleship *Warspite*. The situation looked grim. American planes carried only enough fuel to fight over the beachheads for fifteen minutes.

Also, as army chief of staff General George C. Marshall later pointed out, "The shortage of shipping [much of it already being assembled in Britain for the Normandy landings] made it impossible for General Alexander to bring his own heavy armor into the fight until the British 7th [Armored] Division [along with the U.S. 82d Airborne Division] started to unload on D plus 5 [14 September]."[61]

At this point, General Clark rushed to the front. In an effort to rally his soldiers, he told them: "We don't give another inch. This is it. Don't yield anything. We're here to stay."[62]

At the same time, General Eisenhower informed General Marshall,

> We are very much in the touch-and-go stage of this operation. . . . We have been unable to advance and the enemy is preparing a major counterattack. . . . I am using everything we have bigger

than a rowboat. . . . In the present situation our great hope is the Air Force.[63]

Over the next three days, 12–14 September, General Eisenhower loosed his entire tactical and strategical air forces against the enemy. They delivered. Bombing and strafing, and breaking up enemy columns and troop concentrations, Ike's airpower saved the 5th Army. By nightfall on 15 September, Kesselring began pulling back his forces. The next day, the British 8th Army linked up with the hard-pressed Allied 5th Army about forty miles southeast of Salerno, and the crisis ended.

The 8th Army then seized the vital airfields at Foggia, slightly northeast of Naples near Italy's Adriatic coast, which brought Allied air support right to the edge of the battlefield. Clark's 5th Army, reinforced by the U.S. 3rd Infantry Division, now broke out of the Salerno beachhead and advanced toward Naples. The 5th Army entered the city on 1 October. It lay in smoking ruins—sacked, torched, and booby-trapped by the methodical Germans, who had also sowed the harbor with sunken ships before their departure. Within a month, however, resourceful American engineers had cleared the city and harbor for use as a major supply source for Allied operations farther up the 750-mile-long peninsula.

The Child Warriors

Sandford Africk, a soldier who was severely wounded in the Italian campaign, spent months recovering in a hospital. In the following letter he mailed home, reprinted in William L. O'Neill's *A Democracy at War*, Africk expressed his innermost feelings:

My whole company was replaced except for a handful of lucky men. All my buddies were killed or wounded. At one place I and my squad leader were the only two that were alive and unwounded after the squad was caught in a mortar fire trap. That fellow that I wrote you about that used to hunt chickens and rabbits with me was killed lying next to me. My heart almost broke as I looked at him, but what could I do.

So many buddies gone and so many wounded! My lieutenant got off easy with a scratch on his arm. He is the only officer alive except for the company commander who will have a stiff arm for the rest of his life. Oh, darling, it was hell having my friends falling all around me and all we could do was say goodbye with a salute, and kill more Germans. We walked straight into death, not one man flinched or tried to save himself. I am proud to say, darling, that I was one of the brave lost children. We were all only children after all. The dead boys were cuddled up, the wounded cried for their dead friends. All children, after all.

Raising the Stakes

With the capture of Naples and Foggia, the Allies now held a line across the lower third of the peninsula, but their two-pronged advance began to falter. Field Marshal Kesselring had assured Hitler that he could defend the remaining two-thirds of Italy in a long, open-ended delaying action. To this end, he established a series of defensive lines south of Rome at rivers running crosswise to the peninsula—first the Volturno Line, next the Trigno, then the Sangro, and finally the Garigliano, the Winter Line of 1943–1944. The Winter Line actually consisted of three separate lines—the Barbara Line, the Bernhard Line, and the Gustav Line. Hitler directed the Gustav Line—anchored by the 1,715-foot Monte Cassino—to "mark the end of withdrawals."[64]

Each line bristled with artillery pieces registered on every road, trail, and potential bivouac area. Minefields and demolitions guarded every avenue of approach, along with carefully camouflaged and well-dug-in machine-gun and mortar emplacements. Nature and landscape also collaborated against all Allied attempts to advance.

South of the Po River plain in the far north, the only flat terrain lay in narrow coastal strips, separated by the Apennines—a mountain range of cruel peaks rising to heights of some six thousand feet. Tanks found little room to maneuver, so the task of dislodging the enemy from his rocky heights fell to the foot soldier. The exposed valleys or rivers between each lateral row of rocky pitches had to be traversed under heavy enemy fire. Moreover, the German forces easily obstructed what few good roads existed, demolishing

The Allied Fight for Italy 1943–1944

bridges, sowing mines, and shelling exposed roadways. The cost of taking each ridgeline became appalling, and when Allied troops threatened to surmount one defensive line, the Germans simply retired to another.

Piling misery upon woe, the Italian winter—the worst in several decades—wrapped the battleground in fog, rain, snow, and ice, negating Allied air superiority and rendering roads impassable. After the Salerno campaign, General Montgomery, in a report to British general staff chief Field Marshal Sir Alan Brooke, wrote, "I don't think we can get any spectacular results, so long as it goes on raining; the whole country becomes a sea of mud and nothing on wheels can move off the roads."[65] To add to the Allied difficulties, the Germans were building up their forces faster than the Allies. By December 1943, German divisions in Italy would outnumber those of the Allies twenty to sixteen.

Notwithstanding the heavy odds against them, the Allies decided to raise the stakes in Italy and move against Rome.

Army engineers construct a pontoon bridge over the Volturno River. Weeks of rain had swollen the river to flood level.

The Winter Line Campaign

The Allies resumed their two-pronged offensive in October 1943 and breached the German defenses at the Volturno River, twenty miles north of Naples, beginning the first of many fiercely contested Italian river crossings. Both corps of Mark Clark's 5th Army forded the river—swollen to flood level by weeks of rain—and advanced step by painful step; both corps faced difficult but disparate avenues of advance. The British X Corps moved across flat, open terrain devoid of protective covering; the Allied VI Corps, now commanded by Major General John P. Lucas, clambered over steep hills and trudged along narrow, winding roads, perpetually impeded by blown bridges and blocked culverts. They established a series of bridgeheads at heavy cost before finally gaining control of the Volturno Line on 17 October. In the east, Mont-

gomery's regrouped British 8th Army also resumed its northward march, fording the Trigno River.

By mid-November, the Allied advance had carried to the German Winter Line, commonly referred to as the Gustav Line. After his corps had humped and hammered its way across the mountains north of the Volturno, General Lucas confided to his diary: "I hope I never see another mountain as long as I live."[66] But he would see many more.

The Gustav Line, which Kesselring had prepared well for a stand, was a ten-mile deep defensive zone. It originated on the Gulf of Gaeta, at the mouth of the Garigliano River, coursed along the Rapido, its narrow tributary, then crossed the Apennine spine to the Adriatic, terminating north of the Sangro River. The German 10th Army under General Heinrich von Vietinghoff defended this zone. If the Allies could break through the zone in the Monte Cassino sector, on the Mediterranean side, they would emerge in the wide valley of the Liri River—popularly termed the "Gateway to Rome." From atop Monte Cassino, the great Benedictine abbey—a natural defensive strong point—scowled down on the raging waters of the Rapido below.

On 20 November, Clark's army plunged into this menacing zone, initiating what some call the Winter Line Campaign. Overcoming determined enemy resistance, horribly difficult terrain, and constant rain or snow, they advanced to within five miles of the narrow—but deep and icy—Rapido before the year ended in a blizzardy stalemate on the Winter Line.

Anzio-Rapido Campaign

In December, General Eisenhower, searching for a way to crack the Gustav Line, decided on a new strategy: While Clark's 5th Army pressed a frontal attack against the line, another Allied force would turn Kesselring's front with an amphibious landing at Anzio, about sixty miles north of the stalled Allied left flank and thirty-five miles south of Rome. By threatening Kesselring's line of communications to the Gustav Line, Eisenhower

hoped to force his enemy to either surrender or retire to new positions north of Rome and clear the way for the city's capture. If nothing else, such a move would possibly draw enough German troops away from the Gustav Line to enable Clark's 5th Army to break through into the Liri River Valley and gain a clear path to Rome.

Plans for the operation had barely begun when both Eisenhower and Montgomery returned to England to prepare for the coming offensive in Western Europe. British general Sir Henry M. Wilson assumed overall command in the Mediterranean Theater, and General Sir Oliver Leese took over command of the British 8th Army. The Allied High Command also

GIs clear snow from a tent that has collapsed during a blizzard on the Winter Line.

drew off several veteran divisions from Alexander's 15th Army Group for use in the Normandy landings. A polyglot collection of troops replaced them, including Indian, French, Italian, and New Zealand forces.

General Clark pulled out the VI Corps under General Lucas to execute the Anzio envelopment, code-named Operation Shingle, now set for 22 January 1944. His reorganized 5th Army (six divisions) now comprised the British X Corps, the U.S. II Corps, and the French Expeditionary Corps, made up of hard-fighting Algerian and Moroccan troops.

On 17 January, Clark, as planned, launched a frontal attack against the Gustav Line. The British corps attacked across the Garigliano and gained a bridgehead, while the French corps assaulted the heights north of Cassino. The U.S. 36th Infantry Division (II Corps), under Major General Fred L. Walker, then struck across the Rapido, in the center of the valley's mouth.

The American side of the river was a marshy, mile-wide flood plain without roads. It had been denuded and sown with mines. German mortars and artillery were zeroed in on every inch of it. General Walker held strong reservations about his part of the operation. "I do not know of a single case in military history where an attempt to cross a river that is incorporated into the main line of resistance has succeeded," he noted in his diary. "So I am prepared for defeat."[67] Adding to his difficulties, the British and French failed to gain their objectives, which

meant that his division would lack support on either of its flanks.

Walker's troops started across the Rapido at 2000 on 20 January, blanketed by darkness and heavy fog but under punishing German fire. Those GIs who made it to the far shore were isolated by the enemy and wiped out before dawn. The defending German division reported, "Strong enemy assault detachments, which have crossed the river, are annihilated."[68] In that night alone, the 36th Division lost one thousand men.

Late that afternoon, under an artillery smoke screen, GIs of the 36th tried again. They advanced into withering enemy fire, as later described by Staff Sergeant Bill Kirby, a twenty-two-year-old machine-gun section leader at the time:

> We were under constant fire. I never knew whether they [the attacking troops] made it or not. When we got to the other side, I had never seen so many bodies—our own guys. I remember this one kid being hit by a machine gun; the bullets hitting him pushed him along like a tin can.[69]

Walker's GIs battled throughout the night and well into the next day before the determined German resistance forced them—those who were still alive— back across the Rapido.

In the meantime, while Walker's troops were undergoing the costly defeat he had anticipated, the VI Corps landed unop-

Two GIs are showered with mud kicked up by an exploding German artillery round.

posed at Anzio. General Lucas's corps now consisted of the U.S. 3rd Division, with elements of rangers and paratroopers; with the British 1st Division; and a brigade of commandos. By day's end, Lucas had landed some thirty-six thousand troops and thirty-two hundred vehicles.

Although Anzio and the nearby town of Nettuno fell to the Allies virtually intact, Lucas felt pessimistic about Operation Shingle's chances. "They will end up putting me ashore with inadequate forces and get me in a serious jam," he noted in his diary. "Then, who will take the blame?"[70] The easy answer was that he would, but partly because of his own doing—or lack of it.

Instead of moving inland across Highway 7 to secure the commanding high ground of Alban Hills, Lucas spent the next nine days focusing on unloading more troops and supplies. Meanwhile, Kesselring shifted troops from quiet areas along the Gustav Line—where a stalemate still existed—to build a strong defense perimeter around the Anzio beachhead.

When Lucas finally launched a drive toward Alban Hills on 30 January, Kesselring counterattacked and touched off a furious three-day battle. After both sides incurred about 5,500 casualties, VI Corps fell back and dug in behind a beachhead perimeter of barbed wire and mines. The Germans, now outnumbering Allied troops by about 125,000 to 100,000, launched a second counterattack between 16 and 20 February, but they failed to dislodge the resolute GIs and Tommies.

On 22 February, Clark relieved General Lucas "without prejudice"[71] (because General Alexander had expressed concern over the negative quality of command and the lack of drive and enthusiasm at Anzio) and replaced him with 3rd Division com-

mander Major General Lucian K. Truscott Jr. (It should be noted that General Clark was ashore at Anzio on D day and concurred with Lucas's decision to consolidate forces before driving inland.) The Anzio beachhead entered into a state of siege for the next three months. Now there were two standoffs. And dominating one was Monte Cassino.

Three Battles for Cassino

To the southeast, the 5th Army continued to batter away at the Gustav Line. In the so-called First Battle of Cassino, the U.S. 34th Division continuously assaulted Monte Cassino during the first two weeks of February. The GIs drove to within 400 yards of its 1,715-foot high pinnacle before the Germans finally repulsed them on 12 February.

The Americans' failure to take the heights led to one of the most controversial decisions of the war. Allied leaders suspected (although their suspicions were later disproved) that the Germans were using the historic Abbey of Monte Cassino as an observation post. The abbey, founded by St. Benedict in 529, had been ravaged by conquerors and an earthquake during the Middle Ages. A third catastrophe was soon to befall it. On 14 February, a day commemorating another saint, the Allies dropped leaflets over enemy lines warning,

A German shell explodes near a wave of DUKWs bearing troops and supplies as they approach the beach at Anzio.

Against our will we are now obliged to direct our weapons against the Monastery itself. We warn you so that you may now save yourselves. Leave the Monastery at once.[72]

The next day, 435 Allied bombers—some based as far away as England—dropped 1,000 tons of explosives in the Cassino area, while 750 Allied guns and howitzers shelled the town and the heights behind it with another 4,000 tons of death and destruction. British war correspondent Christopher Buckley, reporting for the *Daily Telegraph*, described the cataclysm:

The ground erupts in smoke, dirt, and rubble as Allied bombers and artillery pound the Cassino area on 15 February.

Sprout after sprout of black smoke leapt from the earth and curled slowly upward like some dark forest. One wave had no sooner started on its return journey than its successor appeared over the eastern skyline. I remember no spectacle so gigantically one-sided. Above, the beautiful, arrogant, silver-grey monsters performing their mission with what looked like a spirit of utter detachment; below, a silent town, suffering all this in complete passivity.[73]

The bombings and shellings raised a wave of protest around the world but failed to achieve any military advantage for the Allies. After the bombardment, German paratroopers moved into the abbey and used the rubble and collapsed beams to establish defensive strong points.

In the Second Battle of Cassino (15–18 February), New Zealand infantry attempted to occupy what remained of the town of Cassino but ran into Germans of the 1st Parachute Division. The paratroopers had resurfaced from refuges in deep tunnels and bunkers. After four days of close-quarter combat, the Germans still held much of the town. In the heights behind Cassino, Indian troops drove to within 250 yards of the abbey, but the paratroopers held fast, forcing the Indians to pull back. A second attack had failed. The Allies would try again.

Following a second air and artillery bombardment that dwarfed the first, the New Zealanders and Indians, augmented this time by the British 78th Division, attacked again on 15 March. But eight days of ferocious fighting ended with the same result. After taking twenty-four hundred casualties, General Alexander called off the Third Battle of Cassino on 23 March. Soon afterward, he shifted most of Leese's British 8th Army from the Adriatic side to the Cassino front, while concentrating the 5th Army along the lower Garigliano River.

Three separate battles failed to wrest the Abbey of Monte Cassino (top of picture) from German control.

Alexander later paid tribute to Cassino's defenders, who had endured such a pounding: "I doubt if there are any other troops in the world who could have stood up to it and then gone on fighting with the ferocity they have." [74]

The Damage Wrought by War

Commencing on 11 May, Alexander brought the entire weight of his 15th Army Group to bear in a surprise, full-scale attack in the twenty-mile zone of the Gustav Line, between Cassino and the sea. In a combined air-ground offensive, American, British, Canadian, French, and Polish troops smashed through the German line and entered the Liri Valley. Kesselring, no longer aided by bad weather, his winter ally, pulled his forces out of the Gustav Line, pivoting them inland and falling back to avoid encirclement. This enabled Polish troops to occupy Cassino (17–18 May) while other Allied troops fought up the Liri Valley (the old Roman Via Caselina) and along Highways 6 and 7—both roads leading to Rome. Young war correspondent Eric Severeid described their progress:

> Always and everywhere the procedure and pattern were the same. German guns betrayed their presence. We called our planes to bomb them. Then we concentrated our artillery, too numerous to be opposed. Thereupon, the infantry flowed slowly ahead. . . . The news would go out to the world that the place was

"liberated." This is the way it was, day after day, town after town.[75]

On 28 May, Truscott's VI Corps plunged through their beachhead perimeter and attacked toward Alban Hills, hoping to cut off great numbers of retreating Germans. General Clark interceded, however, and redirected more than two-thirds of the corps toward Rome, fearful that the rapidly advancing British might slip past the Americans and enter Rome ahead of them. Clark wanted the glory that was Rome for himself. Clark's critics maintain that his self-aggrandizing action permitted most of the Germans retreating from the Gustav Line to escape, which, whether true or not, will never be known. Nonetheless, to the acute displeasure of the British, the Germans *did* escape, and Clark *did* arrive first in Rome, riding in on a jeep on 5 June 1944.

The Italian campaign, from the landing at Salerno to the liberation of Rome, lasted 275 days. It cost the Allied 5th Army 124,917 casualties, including 20,389 dead, 11,292 of whom were American.

General Clark later recalled the jubilance of Rome on its day of liberation:

There were gay crowds in the streets, many of them waving flags, as our infantry marched through the capital. Flowers were stuck in the muzzles of

Advance elements of the VI Corps enter Rome on 4 June 1944. General Clark arrived in the Italian capital the next day, ahead of the British.

the soldiers' rifles and of guns on the tanks. Many Romans seemed to be on the verge of hysteria in their enthusiasm for the American troops. . . . It was on this day that a doughboy [GI] made the classic remark of the Italian campaign, when he took a long look at the ruins of the Colosseum, whistled softly, and said, "Gee, I didn't know our bombers had done that much damage in Rome."[76]

Such jubilance was fleeting, however, and there was little time to assess the damages wrought by war. The Italian campaign would slog on until May 1945. And a day and a half later, the Allies would open a second front in Normandy.

Chapter 5

Operation Overlord: Normandy

"Almighty God—Our sons, pride of our nation, this day have set upon a mighty endeavor, a struggle to preserve our Republic, our religion, and our civilization and to set free a suffering humanity ."
—From President Franklin D. Roosevelt's statement on D day, 6 June 1944 (quoted in Charles B. MacDonald, *The Mighty Endeavor*)

The long-awaited Allied invasion of Western Europe commenced on 6 June 1944—D day—under the overall direction of General Dwight D. Eisenhower, supreme commander of the Allied Expeditionary Force. Although many American strategists had hoped to assault "Fortress Europe" in 1943, the combined Allied forces had lacked sufficient resources—troop strength, air superiority, sufficient landing craft, and logistical support capabilities—for such a large-scale operation until 1944. But now they had them.

Prior to the dawn of 6 June, an armada of some 6,500 Allied naval and transport vessels gathered in the English Channel. At first light, under an umbrella of 12,000-plus aircraft, the Allies began landing 150,000 men on the beaches of Normandy. This massive invasion, code-named Operation Overlord, marked the beginning of the end of Nazi Germany's European domination.

Planning for Overlord

On 12 February 1944, General Eisenhower received a directive from the Combined Chiefs of Staff, officially assigning him to his new, supreme command. "You will enter the Continent of Europe," the directive stated in unvarnished official language, "and, in conjunction with the other United Nations [Allies], undertake

On its way to strike German targets in Normandy, an American bomber flies over ships of the invasion armada. More than 12,000 Allied aircraft took part in Operation Overlord.

operations aimed at the heart of Germany and the destruction of her Armed Forces."[77]

The next day, 13 February, Eisenhower issued his first general order, which established the Supreme Headquarters, Allied Expeditionary Force (SHAEF). A day later, he named his principal subordinates: British air chief marshal Sir Arthur W. Tedder, deputy supreme commander; General Bernard L. Montgomery, top operational commander during the initial phase of the landings and British ground forces commander; Lieutenant General Omar N. Bradley, USA (under Montgomery), com-

mander of U.S. ground forces; British admiral Sir Bertram H. Ramsey, chief of the combined naval forces; and British air chief marshal Sir Trafford Leigh-Mallory, commander of the combined air forces. To Eisenhower and his (and their) subordinates fell the awesome responsibility of planning and directing Operation Overlord. (Planning for the invasion had actually begun on 12 March 1943 under the direction of British lieutenant general Sir Frederick Morgan. The SHAEF planners built on and refined his efforts.)

Targeting an invasion site ranked at the top of SHAEF's agenda. Across the Channel, German defenses stretched from the North Sea coast to the Spanish border. The "Atlantic Wall," as it was called, consisted of a string of recently constructed fortifications and strong points. Minefields and beach obstacles designed to prevent landing craft from beaching filled the wall's defensive gaps. Mines and obstacles were also strewn about inland areas susceptible to airdrops.

Defensive responsibility for the Atlantic Wall belonged to troops of the Western High Command, under Field Marshal K. R.

Once part of the "Atlantic Wall," a massive German gun emplacement stands mute after being neutralized during the invasion.

Gerd von Rundstedt, consisting of ten panzer divisions, fifteen infantry divisions, and thirty-three training or coast-defense divisions (of inferior quality). German troops readily available in the invasion area were the 7th and 15th Armies of Army Group B under Field Marshal Erwin Rommel—four coast-defense divisions, two infantry divisions, the Cherbourg garrison, and three panzer divisions in reserve. Two factors froze the rest of Rommel's troops in place: the disruptive Allied bombing offensive (begun in 1943) and Hitler's obsession with the notion that the Allied thrust would come over the Pas de Calais (Strait of Dover)—the shortest route from England to the Continent.

Because of his obsession with the Pas de Calais, Hitler insisted on concentrating his defensive strength in that area and directed that no panzer divisions be moved without his express orders. Thus, the underdefended Normandy area caught the eye of Allied planners. After carefully weighing their alternatives, the planners targeted Normandy as their invasion site and set D day to fall within the first week of June.

Preparing for Overlord

Over the ensuing months, a massive Allied bombing campaign struck vital bridges, railway yards, and other military and industrial targets in France and Belgium. Meanwhile, the buildup of Allied troops and matériel turned the south of England into an armed camp, in which no fewer than 1,627,000 American GIs and 53,000 sailors assembled and around which a huge armada gathered. Eisenhower called this vast depository of fighting men, ships, and supplies "a great human spring, coiled for the moment when its energy should be released and it would vault the English Channel in the greatest amphibious assault ever assembled."[78]

SHAEF planners overlooked few details that might spell the difference between success or failure in this vast, one-of-a-kind undertaking. Tanks, trucks, guns, rations, barbed wire, and medical supplies were stockpiled, of course. But beyond these ordinary accoutrements of modern warfare, they assembled bulldozers, fleets of buses, railroad locomotives, power plants, entire field hospitals, radio stations, police stations, prison cages, bakeries, laundries, and telephone exchanges, not to mention huge provisions of food, clothing, and fuel, and an ample supply of freshly printed French money. Under way, then, as historian Robert Leckie evocatively suggests, the invasion force would represent "nothing less than a large modern city sailing to battle."[79]

Deception also played an important part in Allied plans and preparations and ultimately in the success of the invasion. As

Prior to sailing across the Channel, men and equipment are loaded aboard LCTs at a British embarkation port.

part of a deception plan called Fortitude, the Allies built an elaborate phony headquarters at Dover, across from Calais, to focus Rundstedt's attention there. Sham equipment, camps (housing troops not scheduled to take part in the initial phase of the Normandy landings), and communications were also concentrated in the Dover area, ostensibly in support of a phantom army under General Patton. (The Germans expected Patton to lead the Allied invasion.) The British leaked misinformation about the "Calais invasion" to known German agents and through intelligence sources monitored the extent to which the Germans were swallowing the bait. Superior Allied air and naval forces prevented German planes and boats from crossing the Channel to see what was *really* happening.

During the last ten days of preparation, the Allies wrapped Britain in a cloak of secrecy. They sealed off all exits to other countries and declared a ten-mile strip of southern England off limits to Britons. These subterfuges paid off handsomely for the Allies. When the time came to execute Operation Overlord, Rundstedt was completely fooled.

Strategies and Objectives

The final invasion plan called for the British 2nd Army to land on beaches just north of Caen and Bayeux, designated Sword, Juno, and Gold. Troops of the U.S. 1st Army were to go ashore at beaches designated Omaha, north of the village of Trévières, and Utah, due east of Sainte-Mère-Église. These landings were set to begin at dawn, preceded several hours earlier by British and American airborne drops at either end of the assault zone.

The objectives of Overlord were several-fold. Once ashore in Normandy, Allied troops were expected to achieve these objectives within three months. First, they were to extend inland and secure a sizable foothold encompassing the region of western France bounded by the Seine and Loire Rivers, along with the Paris-Orleans gap (lower Normandy, all of Brittany, and parts

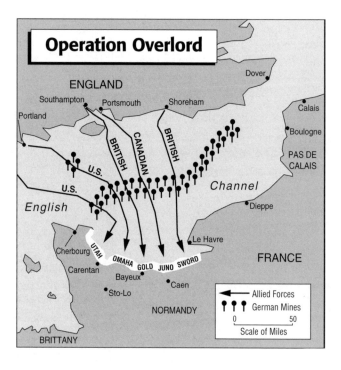

of Maine and Anjou). When established, this lodgment would provide the Allies with ports to sustain and augment their forces; sites for airfields from which to fly ground-support missions; room to maneuver and make full use of their mechanized forces; and space for locating headquarters, installations, replacement and supply depots, and all other facilities essential to modern armies. With these in place, Eisenhower planned to pause and regroup his forces. After reorganizing, he would break out of the enemy's containing armies, attack toward the German border, then smash across the Rhine and into the Ruhr, the heart of German industry.

As June drew near, Eisenhower faced what was perhaps his most difficult decision of the war: setting a date for D day, which depended largely on the cooperation of the weather. A successful landing depended on a calm sea for the invasion ships, a high tide for the landing craft, and a bright moon on the preceding night for the paratroopers. Ike initially picked 4 June 1944, but a storm blew into the Channel and he postponed the landings.

Early on the morning of 5 June, Ike's meteorologist informed him of a brief window of acceptable weather, from late that night until early the next morning, 6 June, when there would be a drop in wind velocity and a break in the cloud cover. Not much of a window, but any further delay would require the naval vessels to refuel, forcing an additional delay of forty-eight hours, still with no assurance of favorable weather. A decision was needed at once. After considering his options (and no doubt the fate of hundreds of thousands of Allied troops) for a full five minutes in silence, Eisenhower said, "O.K. We'll go."[80]

A Place to Start the War

The first elements of airborne assault troops touched down on French soil by

One requirement for the success of Overlord was a bright moon on the night before the landings for the paratroopers (pictured).

parachute and glider shortly after midnight on D day. Their drops lacked the precision called for in their battle plan. Combat correspondent Cornelius Ryan describes the tricky business of jumping at night into a foreign environment:

> Like the British, the U.S. divisions were critically scattered. Only one regiment, the 505th of the 82nd, fell accurately. Sixty percent of all equipment was lost, including most of the radios, mortars, and ammunition. Worse still, many of the men were lost, too. They came down miles from any recognizable landmarks, confused and alone. . . . Hundreds of men, heavily weighted with equipment, fell into the treacherous swamps of Merderet and Douve. Many drowned, some in less than two feet of water. Others, jumping too late, fell into the darkness over what they thought was Normandy and were lost in the Channel.

> One entire stick [group] of 101st paratroopers—some fifteen or eighteen soldiers—met death this way.[81]

At about 0300, some two thousand Allied bombers commenced a two-hour pummeling of German defenses along the landing beaches. Allied warships followed the aerial onslaught with a naval bombard-

Not So Funny

After a predawn airdrop into Normandy on 6 June 1944, U.S. 82nd Airborne commander Major General Matthew B. Ridgway set up headquarters in an apple orchard. In this excerpt from *Eyewitness D-Day*, edited by Jon E. Lewis, Ridgway recounts an episode of questionable hilarity.

The Germans were all around us, of course, sometimes within five hundred yards of my CP [command post], but in the fierce and confused fighting that was going on all about, they did not launch the strong attack that could have wiped out our eggshell perimeter defense.

This was in large part due to the dispersion of the paratroopers. Wherever they landed, they began to cut every communication line they could find, and soon the German commanders had no more contact with their units than we had with ours. When the German commander of the 91st Division found himself cut off from the elements of his command, he did the only thing left to do. He got in his staff car and went out to see for himself what the hell had gone on in this wild night of confused shooting. He never found out. Just at daylight a patrol of paratroopers stopped his car and killed him as he reached for his pistol. The lieutenant commanding the patrol told me the story with great glee.

"Well," I said, "in our present situation, killing division commanders does not strike me as particularly hilarious. But I congratulate you. I'm glad it was a German division commander you got."

ment. A second air attack, this time with one thousand bombers, preceded the landings by fifteen minutes.

The English Channel itself—jammed with invasion vessels of every shape and size imaginable, churned by riotous seas, and swept by piercing winds—posed a scene of wild confusion. Sergeant Malvin Pike of E Company, 2nd Battalion, 8th Infantry, 4th Division, never forgot his wild ride ashore aboard a Higgins boat (a small landing craft named for its inventor):

My position was in the right rear of the boat and I could hear the bullets splitting the air over our heads and I looked back and all I could see was two hands on the wheel and a hand on each .50-caliber machine gun, which the Navy guys were firing. I said to my platoon leader, Lieutenant Rebarcheck, "These guys aren't even looking where they are going or shooting." About that time the coxswain stood up and looked at the beach and then ducked back down. The machine gunners were doing the same and we just prayed they would get us to the beach.

The Higgins boat hit a sandbar as it neared the beach, forcing the infantrymen to wade ashore. Continued Pike,

I jumped out in waist-deep water. We had 200 feet to go to shore and you couldn't run, you could just kind of

push forward. We finally made it to the edge of the water, then we had 200 yards of open beach to cross, through the obstacles [designed to impale landing craft]. . . . What we saw [after scaling the seawall and reaching the top of the sand dunes] was nothing like what we saw on the sand table [mock-up] back in England.[82]

At that point, Brigadier General Theodore Roosevelt Jr., son of the late president and assistant division commander of the 4th Division, joined E Company and determined that they "were not where they were supposed to be." Rather than try to shift the entire landing force about a mile farther down the beach, Roosevelt reportedly said, "We'll start the war from right here."[83] And they did.

The Longest Day

Earlier that morning, at about 0400, Private Franz Gockel stood on the alert at *Widerstandsnest* 62 (WN 62), a German fortification overlooking the Colleville draw at Omaha Beach. While checking on his readiness, Gockel's noncommissioned officer cautioned, "When they come, don't shoot too soon."[84]

At daybreak, Gockel could see the Allied armada in the Channel, seemingly steaming straight at him. "An endless fleet," he recalled. "Heavy warships cruised along as if passing in review." He began fidgeting with his machine gun, checking it over and over again "to take my mind away from impending events." Naval guns started thundering offshore. Gockel went on:

> Salvo after salvo fell into our positions. Debris and clouds of smoke enveloped us. The earth shook. Eyes and ears were filled with dust. Sand ground between teeth. There was no hope for help.
>
> The morning dawn over the approaching landing fleet showed for us our approaching doom. . . . We crouched small and helpless behind our weapons. I prayed for survival.
>
> [Suddenly] the sea came alive. Assault boats and landing craft were rapidly approaching the beach. A comrade stumbled out of the smoke and dust into my position and screamed, "Franz, watch out! They're coming!"[85]

At 0630, in an exchange of cannon fire, an American tank silenced a seventy-five-millimeter cannon at WN 62. Private Franz Gockel settled in for what was shaping up as a very long day.

Several weeks earlier, Field Marshal Erwin Rommel had anticipated this day. On 22 April 1944, he had prophesied to his aide, "Believe me, [Captain Hellmuth] Lang, the

Landing craft pack the shore of Normandy. Above them, barrage balloons tethered by steel cables prevent the Luftwaffe from strafing the beach.

first twenty-four hours of the invasion will be decisive . . . the fate of Germany depends on the outcome. . . . For the Allies, as well as Germany, it will be the longest day."[86] That day had arrived.

Utah Beach

At 0630, the U.S. 4th Infantry Division splashed ashore on Utah Beach, the westernmost of the five landing beaches. By then, paratroopers of the U.S. 82nd and 101st Airborne Divisions had been fighting for hours on the Continent. They had quickly dominated the French countryside inland, as far as seven miles from the beach, and were now engaging enemy troops and taking hostile fire that otherwise would have been directed at the seaborne invaders. Aided by this airborne assist, GIs of the 4th Division quickly established a solid beachhead and drove ten miles inland. The division took fewer than two hundred casualties during the entire first day.

Training paid off at Utah Beach, recalled Sergeant Carwood Lipton of Easy Company, 506th Parachute Infantry Regiment:

We fought as a team without standout stars. We were like a machine. We didn't have anyone who leaped up and charged a machine gun. We knocked it out or made it withdraw by

The U.S. 4th Infantry Division lands on Utah Beach. It was spared from heavy enemy resistance through the efforts of the 82nd and 101st Airborne Divisions.

maneuver and teamwork or mortar fire. We were smart; there weren't many flashy heroics. We had learned that heroics was the way to get killed without getting the job done, and getting the job done was more important.[87]

Sergeant Lipton and about a dozen E Company comrades took on four times their number of elite German paratroopers at a gun battery overlooking the beach. In a superb demonstration of "getting the job done," they wiped out the fifty-man German platoon and neutralized the gun battery. The Americans lost four dead. Two others were wounded.

Sword, Juno, and Gold

On the easternmost beaches—Sword, Juno, and Gold—the day went better than the British and the Canadians had expected but not flawlessly. Because of missed drop zones and mishaps in the glider supply buildup, paratroopers of the British 6th Airborne Division had only partly achieved their objectives of seizing bridges over the Caen Canal and Orne River and knocking out German artillery registered on Sword Beach. Still, at the cost of 650 casualties, the division approximated the success of their American counterparts in easing the landings in the eastern sector.

Troops on these beaches also benefited by an extra hour of naval bombardment, because the difference in tides dictated later landings (0725 at Gold and Juno; ten minutes later at Sword). In one British sector, a company of the Royal Berkshire Regiment experienced one of the day's most surprising receptions. Captain Peter Prior recalls,

> There was a hell of a battle going on further up the beach, but in our sector the opposition quickly crumpled. As we went ashore we were met by a lovely blonde French girl shouting "Vive les Anglais" ["Long live the English"].[88]

This was, of course, an exception. In most instances, the *Wehrmacht* (German army) attended to the welcoming duties, and receptions varied with the caliber of the defending forces. On Gold Beach, for example, the British 1st Hampshire Regiment fought a bitter eight-hour battle with the defenders at Le Hamel; only a few hundred yards to their left, the British Green Howards drove rapidly inland and secured their first objective in under an hour.

Omaha Beach

At Omaha Beach, to the west of Juno, a far different story unfolded. Of the five landing sites, this four-mile-long, crescent-shaped beach was the worst. Commencing in concert with the Utah landings at 0630, the U.S. 1st and 29th Infantry Divisions came ashore at Omaha and immediately collided with the crack German 352nd Infantry Division, which had just

British forces come ashore. At Sword, Juno, and Gold, British and Canadian troops fared better than they had expected.

happened to be pulling maneuvers there. Cornelius Ryan describes the early action:

> They came ashore on Omaha Beach, the slogging unglamorous men that no one envied. . . . They had crossed the beaches of North Africa, Sicily, and Salerno. Now they had one more beach to cross. They would call this one "Bloody Omaha.". . .
>
> [The men at either end of the beach] hadn't a chance. German gunners on the cliffs looked almost directly down on the waterlogged assault craft that heaved and pitched toward these sectors of the beach. Awkward and slow, the assault boats were nearly stationary in the water. They were sitting ducks.
>
> All along Omaha Beach the dropping of the ramps seemed to be the signal for renewed, more concentrated machine-gun fire. . . . But, weighed down by their equipment, unable to run in the deep water and without cover of any kind, men were caught in crisscrossing machine-gun and small-arms fire.[89]

A seventy-man company of rangers lost half its men before it could reach the seawall, three hundred yards from the water. Only twelve remained alive that night. Of sixteen bulldozers meant to clear a path up and over the bluff behind the beach, only

Backs Against the Wall

In the following extract from Juliet Gardiner's *D-Day: Those Who Were There*, Second Lieutenant Charles Cawthon, of the U.S. 29th Infantry Division, describes coming ashore in the second wave at Omaha Beach on D day.

> It was now apparent that we were coming ashore in one of the carefully registered killing zones of German machine-guns and mortars. The havoc they had wrought was all around in an incredible chaos—bodies, weapons, boxes of demolitions, flamethrowers, reels of telephone wire, and personal equipment from socks to toilet articles. Hundreds of brown lifebelts were washing to and fro, writhing and twisting like brown sea slugs. The waves broke around the disabled tanks, bulldozers and beached landing craft that were thick here in front of the heavily defended exit road. . . . The beach rose above me, steep and barren. There was a wide stretch of sand being narrowed by the minute by the [incoming] tide, then a sharply rising shingle bank of small, smooth stones that ended at the sea wall. Against the wall were soldiers of the first assault team. Some were scooping out shelters; a number were stretched out in the loose attitude of the wounded; others had the ultimate stillness of death; but most were just sitting with their backs against the wall. No warlike moves were apparent.

three made it ashore. Able Company of the 116th Regiment landed with 197 men and immediately suffered 96 percent casualties. Its official history recorded, "Within 20 minutes, A Company had become a forlorn little rescue party bent upon survival."[90]

A rain of German steel decimated the three-thousand-man first wave, but the human waves kept coming. Ernest Hemingway, serving as a correspondent on Omaha, wrote, "The first, second, third, fourth, and fifth waves lay where they had fallen, looking like so many heavily laden bundles on the flat pebbly stretch between the sea and the first cover."[91]

Caught between the savage sea and a more savage enemy, the Americans had little choice except to press forward, as clearly illustrated by Colonel Charles Canham's blunt exhortation to his troops. "They're murdering us here," he said. "Let's move inland and get murdered."[92]

Over the course of the morning's action, the German defenders turned Omaha Beach into a smoking disaster area of wrecked landing craft, burned-out tanks, and knocked-out vehicles of every description. Scattered among them lay the smitten, the dying, the dead, and the horror stricken.

At one point, General Bradley, weighing reports of the onshore disasters aboard the cruiser *Augusta*, almost decided to pull his troops off the beach. But early that afternoon, rallied by the courageous leadership of their company commanders and platoon leaders, the GIs rose up and fought back. They advanced methodically, knocking out one enemy position after another, until the entire landing force came together in a wave of irresistible force and swept inland. At 1330, Bradley received this report: "Troops formerly pinned down on beaches Easy Red, Easy Green, Fox Red advancing up heights behind beaches."[93] The crisis had passed on Omaha, the toughest beach, and the success of the Normandy invasion was thereby assured.

Under heavy fire, U.S. troops crawl between obstacles at Omaha Beach. The carnage at Omaha was so great that it was almost decided to abandon the landing.

The Learning Process

By day's end, 6 June 1944, the Allies had landed close to 150,000 troops, along with their accompanying equipment, vehicles, munitions, and provisions. A week later, Allied troops ashore at the Normandy beachhead numbered a half-million men. By late July, the Allies increased their numbers in France to some 2 million men and 250,000 vehicles, aided by the use of prefabricated harbors and floating piers.

One of the soldiers killed on Omaha lies where he fell. His comrades have marked the spot with crossed rifles.

Allied airpower had ruled the skies over Normandy's beaches throughout the invasion operation, limiting the Luftwaffe to fewer than three hundred sorties on D day, compared with 10,585 flown by Allied pilots. At the same time, Allied sea power had sealed off the English Channel from attacks by German submarines and surface vessels.

D day casualty counts for both sides evened out at about 15,000 killed and wounded. During the first forty-eight days of fighting in France, the casualties would mount to 122,000 for the Allies and 117,000 for the Germans.

In the end, the difficulties encountered by the Allies during Operation Overlord tend to validate earlier British fears of invading France prematurely in 1943. Years later, General Bradley concurred:

On reflection, I came to the conclusion that it was fortunate . . . that the U.S. Army first met the enemy on the periphery, in Africa rather than on the beaches of France. In Africa we learned to crawl, then walk—then run. Had the learning process been launched in France, it would surely have . . . resulted in an unthinkable disaster.[94]

The GIs applied their hard-earned knowledge at Normandy and broke out of their beachhead at the end of July. But many obstacles still lay ahead of them on the road to Berlin. One of their greatest tests would come at year's end, on a wooded plateau shared by Belgium, Luxembourg, and France—the Ardennes.

Chapter 6

The Ardennes: The Battle of the Bulge

"I had merely to cross a river, capture Brussels, and then go on and take the port of Antwerp. And all this in the worst months of the year, December, January, February, through the countryside where snow was waist deep and there wasn't room to deploy four tanks abreast, let alone four armored divisions; where it didn't get light until eight in the morning and was dark again at four in the afternoon; with divisions that had just been reformed and contained chiefly raw, untried recruits; and at Christmas time."

—SS colonel general Josef ("Sepp") Dietrich, commander, German 6th SS Panzer Army (quoted in Charles Messenger, *Sepp Dietrich: Hitler's Gladiator*)

War, at best, is bloody and brutal; at worst, it is pure savagery. All too often, savagery ruled on the battlefields of Europe in World War II. One of the war's most renowned and remembered episodes of battlefield barbarity occurred at Baugnez, near the Belgian town of Malmédy, on 17 December 1944. It was the second day of what the Germans later called the Ardennes Offensive and the Allies referred to as the Battle of the Bulge (because the German assault drove a bulge in the Allied line).

Shortly after noon, the advance guard of *Kampfgruppe Peiper* (Battle Group Peiper), a powerful reinforced armored regiment led by *Obersturmbannführer* (lieutenant colonel) Joachim Peiper, overran an American truck convoy just south of Malmédy. Colonel Peiper and his men—members of the elite Waffen-SS (the military arm of Heinrich Himmler's *Schutzstaffel*, or Elite Guard)—were veterans of the eastern front and had a reputation for burning villages and shooting villagers and prisoners of war (POWs).

The Americans belonged to Battery B, 285th Field Artillery Observation Battalion of the 7th Armored Division. Their column was moving southward toward Saint-Vith when Peiper's lead panzer elements roared into it from the east, shooting and generally wreaking havoc among the surprised artillerymen.

The convoy ground to a halt. The Americans dismounted in a wholesale rush to seek cover in roadside ditches or in the nearby forest and were quickly pursued by panzer grenadiers (foot soldiers armed with grenades) who had been riding on the

tanks. Peiper ordered the Americans rounded up and continued his westward drive in the vanguard of the 6th SS Panzer Army.

The Germans captured about 150 Americans and herded them into an open, snow-covered field near the wood. Then a second column of panzers arrived. The Germans positioned a tank at either end of the clearing, bracketing the POWs. Shortly afterward, a command car pulled up with a German officer. He stood up,

A village on the eastern front is set aflame by Nazi storm troopers. Acts of barbarism were all too often committed on the battlefields of Europe.

drew his pistol, took careful aim at an American medical officer in the front rank of prisoners, and fired. When the doctor dropped, the German shot an officer standing beside him. The two tanks then opened fire with their machine guns on the remaining prisoners.

Private Homer Ford, a survivor of the mass slaughter, later testified,

> They started to spray us with machine-gun fire, pistols, and everything. Everybody hit the ground. Then they came along with pistols and rifles and shot some that were breathing and hit others in the head with rifle butts. I was hit in the arm, and of the four men who escaped with me, one was hit in the stomach, and another in the legs.[95]

Some of the Americans escaped into the trees; some feigned death and lived to tell of their ordeal by fire. Seventy of the 150 POWs survived the event that came to be known as the Malmédy Massacre.

Word of the massacre swept through the Allied ranks, and the Americans learned a valuable lesson. On 21 December 1944, an order issued from Headquarters, 328th Infantry Regiment, stated, "No SS troops or paratroopers will be taken prisoner but will be shot on sight."[96] American GIs adapted fast in World War II.

Hitler's Last Gamble

Commencing with the Normandy landings on 6 June, 1944, the Allies moved onto the European continent with some 2.1 million men, shattering German chancellor Adolf Hitler's concept of an impregnable *Festung Europa*—Fortress Europe. By midfall of that year, the Allies had rousted the German defenders back to their own borders at the high cost of some 40,000 Allied killed, 165,000 wounded, and 20,000 missing in action. The Germans fared far worse, incurring a half-million casualties in their field forces and another 200,000 among their coastal defenders. Their bloodied remnants now stood in battered disarray behind the crumbling West Wall, the once-formidable fortified belt along Germany's western frontier, known to the Allies as the Siegfried Line.

Slaughtered American POWs lie in the snow near Malmédy.

Seen here at the beginning of the war, these concrete obstacles of the Siegfried Line were part of Germany's defensive fortifications.

With winter coming on, the German war machine appeared ready to collapse; Germany was on the verge of surrender. But Hitler was planning one last desperate gamble in the hope of snatching victory from the Allied armies swarming at the gates to his Fatherland. He called his ace in the hole the Ardennes Offensive.

On 16 September, 1944, Adolf Hitler summoned Field Marshal Wilhelm Keitel and several top-ranking generals to a special conference at his headquarters, the "Wolf's Lair," near Rastenburg in eastern Germany. In dramatic fashion, he announced, "I have just made a momentous decision. I shall go over to the counterattack!" Jabbing his fin-

ger at a map, he said, "Here, out of the Ardennes, with the objective—Antwerp!"[97]

Insofar as it is possible for one man to draft a major operation, the plan for the Ardennes Offensive belonged solely to Hitler. Almost three months later, on the nights of 11 and 12 December, he finished explaining his offensive to his war leaders:

This battle is to decide whether we shall live or die. I want all my soldiers to fight hard without pity. The battle must be fought with brutality, and all resistance must be broken in a wave of terror.[98]

All participating combatants began assembling on 13 December. Two nights later, twenty reinforced and reequipped German divisions stood poised along a baseline in the forested Eifel region, opposite the Ardennes, with five additional divisions standing in reserve. (The Ardennes, a wooded plateau region east of the Meuse River, covers most of the Belgian province of Luxembourg and part of the Grand Duchy of Luxembourg, and further occupies the Meuse Valley in the French department of Ardennes.) It would seem to even the most casual observer that such a sizable gathering of German troops might stir a ripple of Allied concern. It apparently did not.

Genesis

An old military maxim maintains that surprise can always be achieved by doing something so stupid that it cannot work. Thus Hitler's last-gasp Ardennes Offensive caught the Allies by complete surprise. In December 1944, Allied commanders collectively viewed the idea of a major German offensive as nonsensical; the Germans would achieve nothing by such an attack. The Allies enjoyed superiority on the ground and virtually absolute control of the air and sea. Moreover, the broken, wooded, and hilly terrain of the Ardennes region represented the least likely landscape for an armored attack. Allied leaders dismissed intelligence reports of a possible German attack as impossible. It would be stupid—too stupid to work.

An intelligence report issued by the U.S. 1st Army on 10 December stated, in part, "German strategy in defense of the Reich is based on the exhaustion of our offensive to be followed by an all-out counterattack with armor, between the Rur and the Erft, supported by every weapon he [Hitler] can bring to bear." [99] In the context of this report, Allied strategists considered the term *counterattack* to mean a powerful disruptive attack rather than a major offensive with lasting strategic consequences. In any case, Allied leaders showed no signs of serious concern.

Little suspecting that the Germans would mount a winter offensive, Allied soldiers warm themselves by burning gunpowder from their artillery shells.

Two days later, on 12 December, Lieutenant General Omar N. Bradley's U.S. 12th Army Group intelligence chief reported,

It is now certain that attrition [a gradual wearing down or depletion of troops and resources] is steadily sapping the strength of German forces on the Western Front and that the crust of [German] defenses is thinner, more brittle and more vulnerable than it appears in our G-2 [intelligence] maps or to the troops in the line. [100]

The newly promoted field marshal Bernard L. Montgomery concurred. The G-2 section of his Anglo-Canadian 21st

Army Group reported that the enemy was "at present fighting a defensive campaign on all fronts; his situation is such that he cannot stage a major offensive operation."[101]

These assessments of the enemy's military capabilities were based on the assumption that they were dealing with the rational thinking of the conventional German militarist, but they were not. Instead, they were contending with the half-crazed aberrations of Hitler. Hitler had taken personal control over the German army after a failed attempt to assassinate him during the previous July. Because several regular army commanders had been implicated (and later executed) in the plot to kill him, Hitler had grown to place increasing trust in the Waffen-SS, the Nazi Party's own armed forces. It was to the Waffen-SS that he entrusted the execution and success of his Ardennes Offensive, an operation as reckless and daring as it was unpredictable. He initially called it *Wacht am Rhein*, or Watch on the Rhine (a defensive-sounding name intended to deceive the Allies if they were somehow to hear of it). The name was later changed to *Herbstnebel*, or Autumn Mist.

Hitler was probably mad but certainly not stupid. As 1944 drew to a close, he knew that the war had been lost—unless he could find a way to break up the Big Three alliance of Britain, the Soviet Union, and the United States. But how?

Hitler wondered. Only by desperate measures, he decided. If he could force Britain and the United States into a negotiated peace, Germany might remain strong enough to overcome the Soviets in the east.

Briefly, his strategy called for a whirlwind attack by Field Marshal Walther Model's Army Group B, made up of reserve armies of 250,000 men and 1,100 tanks. The 6th SS Panzer Army under SS colonel general Josef ("Sepp") Dietrich and the 5th Panzer Army under General Hasso-Eccard von Manteuffel were to strike along a seventy-five-mile front stretching from Monschau south to Echternach, which was thinly defended by Major General Troy H. Middleton's U.S. 8th Corps.

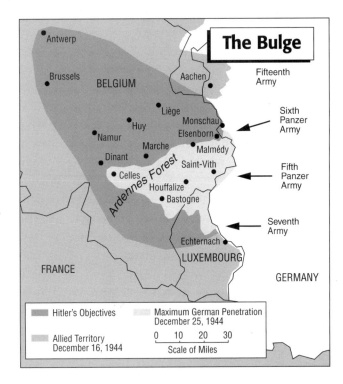

The Bulge

Antwerp

Brussels

BELGIUM

Aachen

Fifteenth Army

Liège

Monschau

Sixth Panzer Army

Huy

Namur

Elsenborn

Marche

Malmédy

Dinant

Ardennes Forest

Saint-Vith

Fifth Panzer Army

Celles

Houffalize

Bastogne

Seventh Army

Echternach

LUXEMBOURG

FRANCE

GERMANY

Hitler's Objectives

Maximum German Penetration December 25, 1944

Allied Territory December 16, 1944

0   10   20   30

Scale of Miles

They were to attack in bad weather to neutralize Allied airpower. With General Erich Brandenberger's 7th Army protecting their southern flank, they would drive to the Meuse River in two days and secure bridgeheads. In the next two days, with Dietrich spearheading and Manteuffel supporting, they would press on to recapture the Belgian cities of Liège and Antwerp, both Allied supply bases. While doing so, they were to slice Eisenhower's forces in half and destroy the Allied armies (the Canadian 1st, British 2nd, U.S. 9th, and most of the U.S. 1st Armies) lying north of a line drawn through Bastogne-Brussels-Antwerp.

If this desperate gamble paid off, the offensive would effectively destroy the Anglo-Canadian armed forces, leaving the weakened Americans to fight on alone against the Japanese in the Pacific. With the Americans so preoccupied, Hitler reasoned, they might prefer a negotiated peace to the prospect of a Europe dominated by a victorious Soviet Union. Hitler's reasoning, however, was wrong. The Big Three alliance not only held together but grew stronger as the war wore on. Yet Hitler persisted with his fantasy, and the ill-conceived fruits of his deranged passions became all too real in the Battle of the Bulge.

"Wave of Terror"

Hitler's Ardennes Offensive started at 0530 on 16 December 1944 with a 2-hour bombardment by two thousand guns of German Army Group B, which caught the Americans completely by surprise. When the artillery barrage lifted, three German armies, amid fog and a freezing snow, plunged into the Ardennes forests of Belgium and Luxembourg. Sepp Dietrich's 6th SS Panzer Army spearheaded the attack in the north, with Manteuffel's 5th Panzer Army in the center and Brandenberger's 7th Army to the south.

Lieutenant General Courtney H. Hodges's U.S. 1st Army, part of Bradley's 12th Army Group, was responsible for the Ardennes, but most of his strength lay in the Aachen area, where he was driving to capture the Rur dams. The Ardennes was a quiet sector chosen for new or recuperating divisions, and only five defended the seventy-five-mile front: the 99th and 106th Infantry Divisions from Hodges's 5th Corps; the 28th and 4th Infantry Divisions from his 8th Corps, and the 9th Armored Division in reserve.

The twenty-division German assault shattered the U.S. 106th and 28th Infantry Divisions and the 9th Armored Division—ranging, respectively, from the central to the southern sector of the Allied front—and sent them reeling back in disarray. (The green troops of the 106th had just arrived at the front, and the 28th was still recovering from severe fighting earlier at Schmidt, just north of the Rur River dams.) The Germans achieved surprise and penetration along the so-called Ghost Front, creating the "bulge" that gave its name to the battle, but failed to break through.

American GIs, even though surrounded in some areas, held on and fought hard—in deep snow and freezing temperatures. Major General Heinz Kokott, whose 26th Volksstrum Division attacked the U.S. 28th Division east of Bastogne, later commended the GIs of the 28th:

German assault troops race past abandoned Allied equipment on the "Ghost Front." The Ardennes Offensive caught the Americans completely by surprise.

What had not been expected to such an extent was the way that the remnants of the beaten units of the 28th did not give up the battle. They stayed put and continued to block the road. Fighting a delaying battle . . . individual groups time and again confronted our assault detachments from dominating heights, defiles, on both sides of gullies and on forest paths. They let the attacking parties run into their fire, engaged them in a fire duel, made evading movements with great skill and speed and then conducted unexpected counterthrusts into flanks and rears.[102]

"Glorious Hours and Days"

In a letter dated 22 December 1944, Lieutenant Rockhammer of the German army describes the ambush of an American truck convoy at the height of the German advance in the Ardennes. The following extract appears in *The War, 1939–1945*, edited by Desmond Flower and James Reeves.

This time we are a thousand times better off than you at home. You cannot imagine what glorious hours and days we are experiencing now. It looks as if the Americans cannot withstand our important push. To-day we overtook a fleeing column and finished it. We overtook it by taking a back-road through the woods to the retreat lane of the American vehicles; then, just like on maneuvers, we pulled up along the road with sixty Panthers [tanks]. And then came the endless convoy driving in two columns, side by side, hub on hub, filled to the brim with soldiers. And then a concentrated fire from sixty guns and one hundred and twenty machine-guns. It was a glorious bloodbath, vengeance for our destroyed homeland. Our soldiers still have the old zip. The snow must turn red with American blood. Victory was never as close as it is now.

At day's end, as a result of delaying actions and stronger resistance by the U.S. 5th Corps on the north flank and the U.S. 4th Infantry on the south flank, the Germans had failed to secure any of the crossroads—principally at Bastogne and Saint-Vith—that would enable their tanks to roam free behind the American lines. A German decision to hold back their tanks until the infantry broke through was proving to be a major tactical error.

Confusion reigned all along the front during the first day's action. Hitler compounded the confusion with another of his brainchildren, this one called Operation Grief (Griffen). A special Nazi unit of English-speaking Germans, led by SS colonel Otto Skorzeny, infiltrated the American lines dressed as Americans in American vehicles. They began at once misdirecting traffic and transmitting misinformation over the radio. At times, the Americans could not tell a GI from a German. Operation Grief spread panic and confusion in the Allied ranks but did not affect the battle's outcome.

Hitler also ordered a parachute drop of some one thousand paratroopers under Colonel Friedrich von der Heydte near Malmédy. Heydte's orders were to block off Allied reinforcements attempting to enter the Ardennes from the north. Strong headwinds and antiaircraft fire en route to the drop zone resulted in a widely scattered airdrop and a failed mission. But the paratroopers contributed greatly to the confusion factor.

When SS lieutenant colonel Joachim Peiper's panzers arrived at the village of Lanzerath after midnight, Peiper learned that the advance of an entire battalion of the German 3rd Parachute Division had been held up all day by a gallant U.S. infantry platoon under Lieutenant Lyle J. Bouck Jr. The paratroop commander explained to Peiper that his troops failed to break through because "the woods up the way were full of Americans."[103] Peiper turned livid with rage.

At 0400 the next morning, *Kampf-gruppe Peiper* embarked on a killing spree that embodied the spirit of Hitler's edict "to fight hard without pity" and to fight "with brutality," breaking all resistance "in a wave of terror." Peiper's battle group roared up the road and attacked the next villages—Honsfeld, Büllingen, Baugnez— capturing and killing GIs by the dozens. Their blood lust reached its zenith at the Belgian town of Malmédy, where they captured 150 GIs of Battery B, 285th Field Artillery Observation Battalion of the 7th Armored Division, and slaughtered eighty of them. Word of the massacre spread quickly, electrifying frontline GIs and stiffening their resolve. After Peiper's wave of terror, several American units pledged to take no prisoners wearing an SS uniform. And they did not.

The Meaning of "Nuts!"

While the panzers clanked westward, General Eisenhower, at SHAEF in Versailles, told his subordinates, "The present situation is to be regarded as one of opportunity for us and not of disaster."[104] The Germans had abandoned their defensive fortifications and in so doing had made themselves vulnerable to attack. After consulting his commanders, Ike acted swiftly and decisively. He ordered the 10th Armored Division of Lieutenant General George S. Patton's U.S. 3d Army, south of the Ardennes, and the 7th Armored Division of Lieutenant General William H. Simpson's U.S. 9th Army, to the north of Hodges, to reinforce the frontline divisions.

U.S. soldiers take position in the Belgian woods. During the offensive, one American infantry platoon halted an entire German parachute division.

The reinforcements came just in time. With Hodges's frontline forces in the north and south hanging on by a thread, the first three days of the German assault were the most critical. Ike further bolstered the 99th Division in the north with the 1st and 2nd Divisions and later with the 9th. These divisions blocked Sepp Dietrich's 6th SS Panzer advance around the Elsenborn Ridge, east of Malmédy, while in the south the U.S. 4th Division contained the thrust of Brandenberger's *Volksgrenadier*. Although the anchors on both flanks of the American line held firm, the 28th and 106th Divisions in the center collapsed against the surge of Manteuffel's 5th Panzers. The panzers tore through a thirty-mile gap between Saint-Vith and Bastogne and headed for the two important crossroads in the local road network.

The Germans isolated two regiments of the 106th Division and forced the surrender of some seven thousand troops. Except for Bataan, it was the largest American capitulation of the war. But a third regiment of the 106th, along with the 7th Armored Division under Brigadier General Robert W. Hasbrouck, mounted a stout defense in front of Saint-Vith. Despite innumerable American heroics, the German onslaught forced the GIs to withdraw from the horseshoe-shaped defense perimeter and retire to the Salm River on 22 December.

By then, Eisenhower had turned over field command of the northern forces to Field Marshal Montgomery, while the southern forces remained under General Bradley. With Manteuffel closing fast on Bastogne, Ike pulled the 101st Airborne Division out of reserve and sent it racing to help the 10th Armored Division, and fragments of other commands under Brigadier General Anthony C. McAuliffe, hold the town.

McAuliffe's forces beat Manteuffel's crack 2nd Panzer Division to Bastogne by only hours. But when the 2nd Panzers arrived on 19 December, they were ordered to continue their dash toward the Meuse

A German panzer drives past a column of American troops taken prisoner during the Battle of the Bulge.

and leave the capture of the town to General Kokott's 26th *Volksgrenadiers* and Major General Fritz Bayerlein's Panzer Lehr (Tank Demonstration) Division.

Bayerlein had told his officers that this offensive would determine the war's outcome. He had placed himself at the head of his advanced guard, stating, "It's not important whether I'm killed."[105] His men sensed in their commander a ruthless will to win and adopted it as their own. On 20 December, German troops encircled Bastogne from the north and south and spent the next two and a half days massing for an attack.

At the same time, Eisenhower, hoping to relieve some of the pressure on Hodges (and Bastogne), ordered Patton to swing his 3rd Army's advance axis ninety degrees and attack the bulge from the south. Patton complied with extraordinary swiftness and precision. In the north, Montgomery shifted his reserve British 30th Corps between Liège and Louvain, while Hodges, in another amazing show of American mobility, realigned his 7th Corps for counterattack at the opportune time. Meanwhile, McAuliffe's holdout at Bastogne continued to slow Manteuffel's advance.

At 1130 on 22 December, four Germans carrying a white flag advanced on McAuliffe's company command post bearing a request from the German commander. It stated that the Americans should either surrender or face annihilation by German artillery. After conferring with his staff, McAuliffe scribbled this reply:

To the German Commander:
Nuts!
—The American Commander

Colonel Joseph Harper, commander of the U.S. 327th Glider Infantry Regiment, volunteered to deliver the message himself. "It will be a lot of fun," he said. When a German asked what the message meant, Harper snapped, "If you don't understand what 'Nuts' means, in plain English it's the same as 'Go to Hell.'"[106] A furious five-day battle ensued, but the besieged GIs did not yield an inch.

Brigadier General Anthony McAuliffe had a simple reply when asked by the Germans to surrender the town of Bastogne: "Nuts!"

On the afternoon of 26 December, the spearheading units of Patton's 4th Armored Division drew within four miles of Bastogne. Colonel Creighton W. Abrams, commander of the 37th Tank Battalion and a future chief of staff of the U.S. Army, radioed his headquarters to authorize a direct attack on the town. Patton replied, "I sure as hell will!"[107]

Shortly after 1500, Abrams stuffed a cigar in his mouth and said from the turret of his tank, "We're going in to those people now. Let 'er roll!"[108] And so they rolled, crushing the German attackers in their path and lifting the siege of Bastogne. McAuliffe's intrepid troops now belonged to Patton's 3rd Army. And "Nuts!" became their creed.

"La Gleize's Expendables"

Combatants on both sides of the fighting at Bastogne and all across the Ardennes reached a ferocity and single-minded purposefulness unsurpassed by warriors of any

---

A Good Situation

Correspondent Martha Gellhorn visited Bastogne right after the German siege was lifted. The following is an excerpt from her article "The Battle of the Bulge," which is reprinted in the Library of America's *Reporting World War II.*

You have seen Bastogne and a thousand other Bastognes in the newsreels. These dead towns are villages spread over Europe and one forgets the human misery and fear and despair that the cracked and caved-in buildings represent. Bastogne was a German job of death and destruction and it was beautifully thorough. The 101st Airborne Division, which held Bastogne, was still there, though the day before the wounded had been taken out as soon as the first road was open. The survivors of the 101st Airborne Division, after being entirely surrounded, uninterruptedly shelled and bombed, after having fought off four times their strength in Germans, look—for some unknown reason—cheerful and lively. A young lieutenant remarked, "The tactical situation was always good." He was very surprised when we shouted with laughter. The front, north of Bastogne, was just up the road and the peril was far from past.

After the siege of Bastogne, an American soldier stands next to a truck overturned by German shellfire.

other time or place. Captain Edward McBride, of Somerset, Kentucky, did not fully grasp the determination and gallantry exhibited by a company of American GIs near La Gleize, Belgium, until after their positions had been lost and regained. On 29 December 1944, in the lull after battle, McBride told the story of "La Gleize's expendables" to International News Service staff correspondent Frank Conniff:

When I would come to an American machine-gun position, I'd find all the ammunition gone. Then I'd see the gunners. They would have carbines and pistols still clutched in their hands. I'd pry a weapon loose and find all its chambers empty. Occasionally, there would be one or two cartridges left.

All around them would be dead Germans. Our men kept fighting until everything was gone, using pistols when nothing else was left.

Then I'd go to the mortar position and find the same story. I'd see dead GIs still holding rifles. Some had knives, but they just kept fighting till the last bullet. All around them would be dead Jerries [Germans].

Everywhere I'd find dead Americans—lots of them—I'd find a dozen dead Nazis sprawled around each of them.[109]

Correspondent Conniff ended his dispatch from the front this way:

In future years when hoary Junkers weigh the imponderables of this blazing struggle, they might remember McBride and the men of La Gleize.

For not in maps or statistics will they find the answer to what happened here. It was something in our heritage. Something that happened a long time ago. Something only an American could understand.[110]

During the Battle of the Bulge there were countless acts of extraordinary American heroism and, as in all battles, a lesser number of cowardly deeds. Not every soldier was a hero—only most of them.

As a sidebar to the action at La Gleize, *Kampfgruppe Peiper*'s tanks ran out of fuel in that vicinity and became entrapped by the U.S. 82nd Airborne Division. Peiper's men either dispersed and escaped or surrendered. After the war, Peiper himself was convicted of war crimes by an Allied tribunal and sentenced to hanging.

Hastening the End

Perhaps the unsung heroes of the Bulge were the men of the Allied air forces. Their importance cannot be overstated, for they shattered the already inadequate German supply groups and further delimited the mobility of the panzers, which were already restrained by fuel shortages, poor roads, dogged Allied resistance, and the narrowness of their front.

Late on 22 December, just as the battle for Bastogne commenced, the skies had begun to clear. The next day, the U.S. 9th Air Force flew thirteen hundred sorties. And on Christmas Eve, two thousand Allied aircraft attacked thirty-one separate targets in the Ardennes sector. Their efforts provoked a mass response by the Luftwaffe on New Year's Day, 1945.

Hitler called the massive air attack "the Great Blow." He intended to abolish the Allied airpower that was proving so lethal over the Ardennes. Starting at 0800, hundreds of German aircraft struck 27 Allied airfields scattered across Belgium, Holland, and northern France. They demolished 156 Allied aircraft, but at the unaffordable loss of 300 of their own. More important, they lost 253 experienced pilots. The losses sounded the Luftwaffe's death knell, for it never took to the air again in significant numbers.

While the battle for Bastogne still raged, the 2nd Panzer Division's thrust toward the Meuse ground to a halt when the panzers ran out of fuel near Celles, within sight of the river. The bulge, now sixty miles deep and forty miles wide at its base, had reached its maximum penetration. On 3 January, an American pincer, formed by Hodges's 1st Army in the north and Patton's 3rd Army in the south, began squeezing the bulge. Deep snow conditions

delayed the two pincers from closing on Houffalize until 16 January, however, and the Germans, more accustomed to the snow, managed to escape. By 28 January, the Americans had reclaimed all of their lost territory, and the Battle of the Bulge ended.

Hitler had gambled and lost. The loss cost the Germans almost 120,000 casualties, 600 tanks and assault guns, 1,600 aircraft, and 6,000 vehicles. Allied losses (mostly American) totaled almost 20,000 killed, 40,000 wounded, 21,000 captured or missing, and some 730 tanks and tank destroyers. Summarily, although the battle had delayed the Allied advance into Germany by about six weeks, Hitler had expended irreplaceable resources of troops and equipment that could have been used to check the impending Soviet spring offensive.

Before the battle, Hitler had told armaments and war production minister Albert Speer that Autumn Mist would "lead to collapse and panic among the Americans" and that the Germans would "drive right through their middle and take Antwerp." In reality, as Speer wrote later, "The failure of the Ardennes offensive meant that the war was over."[111]

Hitler's losses in the Ardennes certainly hastened the end of the war in Europe. But for American GIs and their comrades in arms, the last battles were still to be fought.

Chapter 7

Remagen and the Race to Berlin

"We ran down the middle of the bridge, shouting as we went. My men were in squad column and not one of them was hit."
—Sergeant Alexander Drabik, Company A, 27th Armored Infantry Battalion (quoted in Norman Polmar and Thomas B. Allen, eds., *World War II*)

After hammering the "bulge" back to their original line of eastward advance, the Allies resumed operations to clear the west bank of the Rhine on 8 February 1945. In the 21st Army Group sector to the north, Field Marshal Montgomery launched a pincers maneuver: General Henry Crerar's Canadian 1st Army attacked southeasterly between the Meuse and the Rhine Rivers (Operation Veritable), while General Simpson's U.S. 9th Army attacked across the Rur on 23 February (Operation Grenade). The two armies converged at Geldern on 3 March. By 10 March, the Canadians had wiped out the last German bridgehead, opposite Wesel, and Montgomery's armies stood on the Rhine.

Montgomery wanted to cross the Rhine independently and drive across the northern plains to Berlin, confident that he could beat the Soviets to the German capital and thereby alter the map of postwar Europe. But Eisenhower restrained Montgomery, insisting on crossing the Rhine and advancing on a broad front, a sounder military strategy.

Surprisingly, some strategists have criticized Ike for not freeing Montgomery. Historian John Ellis, one of many Ike supporters, disdains such criticism. "The more surprising, it seemed, [is] that anyone really believed that the man that waddled tortoise-like behind Rommel in North Africa, who traversed Sicily and [Italy] with if anything more circumspection [caution], should suddenly have been transformed into a dashing amalgam of Frederick the Great and Jeb Stuart."[112] Eisenhower, quite correctly, insisted on maintaining his broad-front policy.

South of Montgomery, in General Bradley's 12th Army Group sector, General Hodges's U.S. 1st Army protected Simpson's right flank. Hodges pressed through the Hürtgen Forest and drove for the Rhine, rolling back Manteuffel's 5th Panzer Army and the remnants of General Gustav von Zangen's 15th Army in his path. Elements of the 1st Army swept across the Rhine plain and cleared Cologne (6–7 March), while, to the south, elements of Patton's 3rd Army punched their way through the West Wall, north of the Moselle River.

Meanwhile, General Bradley, using the rest of the 1st and 3rd Armies in the central sector, launched a broad attack toward the middle Rhine (Operation Lumberjack) on 5 March. Over the next five days, they advanced to the river from Koblenz, traveled northward through Bonn and Cologne, and then linked up with the Canadians at Wesel.

While Field Marshal Montgomery wanted to race the Soviets to Berlin, General Eisenhower insisted that the Allies advance on a broader front.

The Bridge at Remagen

Through a breach in the Siegfried Line, elements of Patton's 3rd Army cross into Germany.

The rapid American advance to the Rhine yielded a surprise dividend of inestimable value. Task Force Engeman, an armored patrol of Hodges's 1st Army, broke into the town of Remagen, near Bonn. To their amazement, they discovered the Ludendorff Railway Bridge still standing, still spanning the robust waters of the Rhine.

The task force immediately notified Combat Command B (CCB) commander Brigadier General William M. Hoge of their discovery. Hoge rushed to the scene. After surveying the situation, Hoge turned to task force commander Lieutenant Colonel Leonard Engeman and said, "I want you to get to that bridge as soon as possible."[113]

"Already on their way,"[114] came the reply.

Engeman had already sent GIs of Second Lieutenant Karl Timmerman's Company A into town. While they paused on the west bank of the bridge, the Germans on the east bank tried to blow up the bridge with previously implanted demolitions. But a shell had severed an ignition wire to a five-hundred-pound charge of TNT, so their

From the shelter of a railway tunnel, Allied soldiers survey the bridge at Remagen. Troops and vehicles would soon use the bridge to cross the Rhine.

attempt failed. Shortly afterward, assistant squad leader Sergeant Alex Drabik raced across the bridge and took cover in a shell crater. He was the first Allied soldier to cross the Rhine. Eight members of his squad darted right after him. Within ten minutes, one hundred GIs had sped across, including Timmerman, the first officer to cross.

In war, great decisions are often made—and the tides of battle often turn—on chance and happenstance, and here was a textbook case. When news of the fortuitous seizure reached General Omar Bradley at his 12th Army Group headquarters, he phoned 1st Army commander General Courtney Hodges and shouted, "Hot Dog, Courtney, this will bust 'em wide open. Shove everything you can across!"[115] Hodges complied and expanded the bridgehead on the east side of the river.

When Bradley notified Eisenhower of the 1st Army's chance discovery, Ike said, "Brad, that's wonderful." And when Bradley informed him that he wanted to push four divisions across, Eisenhower replied, "Sure, get right on across with everything you've got. It's the best break we've had." In fact, Ike authorized Bradley to put five divisions into the bridgehead if needed. "Make sure you hold that bridgehead," he said. Bradley then told Ike that SHAEF's operations chief opposed expanding the bridgehead. Ike replied strongly, "To hell with the planners. Sure, go on, Brad, and I'll give you everything we've got to hold that bridgehead."[116]

Thus Ike countermanded his broad-front policy, however temporarily, to take advantage of a fortuitous opportunity. He changed his battle plans and ordered all available troops to head for Remagen. "This was one of my happy moments of the war,"[117] he said later. For the next ten days, a steady stream of troops and vehicles poured across the bridge.

When Hitler learned that the bridge at Remagen had not been demolished, he became so incensed that he fired Field Marshal Gerd von Runstedt and replaced him with Field Marshal Albert Kesselring. Hitler unleashed all available weaponry against the bridge, including artillery, V-2 rockets, and the new Me 262 jet fighter-bomber. The bridge finally collapsed without warning on 17 March, killing twenty-seven Americans. But by then, GI engineers had constructed numerous pontoon bridges and five divisions had crossed the bridge at Remagen.

Commenting on the operation later, army chief of staff General George C. Marshall said, "The prompt seizure and exploit of the crossing demonstrated American initiative and adaptability at its best, from the daring action of the platoon commander to the Army commander who quickly redirected all his moving columns in a demonstration of brilliant staff management."[118] In short, well done all.

In his attempt to destroy the bridge at Remagen, Hitler unleashed V-2 rockets (above) and Me 262 fighter-bombers (right). The Me 262 was the first operational jet fighter.

The Quality of Mercy

Occasionally, in the throes of mortal combat, an unexpected display of human decency helps restore some sense of sanity in an otherwise crazed existence. After an incident near Remagen in which some German soldiers had captured a group of American medics and treated them with great civility, GIs of the 9th Infantry Division returned their kindness. Foot soldier Don Lavender of the 9th recalls,

> Three of us were selected to make a jeep patrol to check a bridge about two miles away. [After seeking directions at a nearby farmhouse, they found the bridge intact and then returned to the farmhouse.] While [there], we spotted a German soldier in the woods and when we ordered him to come to the house, we discovered he was a medical officer. He told us there were more in the woods and they had two trucks, but were out of gas. Our jeep driver made a special trip for gas and when all of them came out there were 43 including several nurses. At last report, our regiment had returned them to the Germans because of the German shortage of medics.[119]

Whenever possible, both sides routinely followed the practice of returning medical personnel and chaplains to their respective ranks at the earliest opportunity. Such was the occasional unstrained quality of mercy in the shadow of unrestrained violence and brutality.

Eisenhower Bears Witness

The Allies were soon to experience grim evidence of the darker side of their enemy. On 13 April the first British tanks entered the Nazi death camp at Belsen and discovered unspeakable horrors. Patrick Gordon-Walker, a British officer, later described the gruesome scene that greeted their entrance:

> People were falling dead all around— people who were walking skeletons. . . . One woman came up to a soldier who was guarding the milk store and doling out milk to children, and begged for milk for her baby. [The man saw that it had been dead for days but poured milk on its lips to humor her.] The mother then started to croon with joy and carried the baby off in triumph. She stumbled and fell dead in a few yards.[120]

The British counted some thirty-five thousand corpses at Belsen, five thousand more than the living inmates. The Allies discovered similar horrors in other concentration and extermination camps scattered throughout Germany and Nazi-held territories.

When Eisenhower learned of such death camp atrocities, he personally visited a camp at Ohrdruf to see for himself. He said that he had gone "in order to be in a position to give first-hand evidence of these

Seeking Out the Living

As the American armies advanced into Germany, the GIs were "stunned, horrified and sickened" to discover Nazi atrocities at German slave labor camps. In *A General's Life*, Omar N. Bradley and Clay Blair recall one army medic's reaction to a camp at Nordhausen:

> Rows upon rows of skin-covered skeletons met our eyes. Men lay as they had starved, discolored, and lying in indescribable filth. Their striped coats and prison numbers hung to their frames as a last token or symbol of those who enslaved and killed them. . . . One girl in particular I noticed: I would say she was about seventeen years old. She lay there where she had fallen, gangrened and naked. In my own thoughts I choked up—couldn't quite understand how and why war could do these things. . . . We went downstairs to a filth indescribable, accompanied by a horrible dead-rat stench. There in beds of crude wood I saw men too weak to move dead comrades from their side. One hunched-down French boy was huddled up against a dead comrade, as if to keep warm. . . . There were others, in dark cellar rooms, lying in disease and filth, being eaten away by diarrhea and malnutrition. It was like stepping into the Dark Ages to walk into one of these cellar cells and seek out the living.

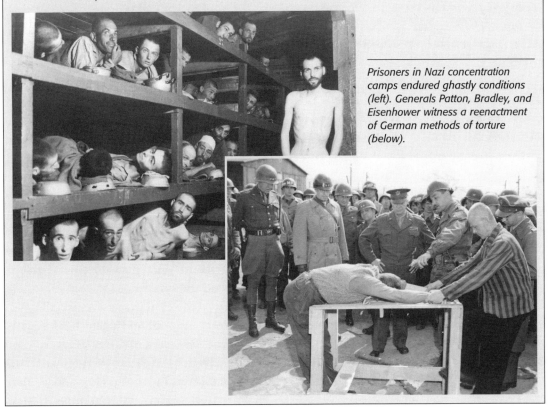

Prisoners in Nazi concentration camps endured ghastly conditions (left). Generals Patton, Bradley, and Eisenhower witness a reenactment of German methods of torture (below).

things if ever in the future there develops a tendency to charge these allegations to propaganda."[121] By bearing witness to such atrocities, Eisenhower displayed wisdom and a vision of the future, for today some history revisionists try to deny that the atrocities ever occurred.

The Final Offensive

By 26 March, the entire Allied front had moved across the Rhine, and German defenses were collapsing. At the same time, the Soviet armies were advancing swiftly westward, steamrolling over German resistance, intent on beating the Western Allies to Berlin. As many GIs perceived it, the race was on. But to the chagrin of many GIs and officers, Eisenhower restored his broad front policy.

From 11 to 21 March 1945, General George S. Patton's 3rd Army drove southeast across the Moselle River, while General Alexander M. Patch's 7th Army attacked northeast from the Saar River. With control of the skies overhead, the two armies joined in a superbly coordinated crisscrossing attack and eradicated the dazed elements of General Erich Brandenberger's German 7th Army.

Action in the Rhineland cost the Germans some 60,000 killed or wounded, and 250,000 were taken prisoner. The Allies, who also commandeered great quantities of matériel, took fewer than 20,000 casualties in dead and wounded. The war in the European Theater now entered its final phase.

On 28 March, with his forces aligned to the east of the Rhine, Eisenhower ordered Bradley's 12th Army Group to make the main Allied advance on a three-army front along the axis Kassel-Mühlhausen-Leipzig. He further ordered Montgomery's 21st Army Group to protect Bradley's left (north) flank and attack through the Netherlands and northern Germany. Last, he ordered Lieutenant General Jacob L. Devers's 6th Army Group to protect Bradley's right (south) flank in southern Germany. Bradley's 1st (Hodges) and 3rd (Patton) Army armored units now plunged northeast, averaging thirty miles a day.

On 12 April, President Franklin D. Roosevelt died of a massive cerebral hemorrhage at his home in Warm Springs, Georgia. While battle-hardened GIs wept at the news of his death, Nazi propaganda minister Joseph Goebbels said, "This is the turning point."[122] He meant for the Nazis, and he could not have been more wrong. The Soviets took Vienna the next day and were closing fast on Berlin.

In mid-April, the U.S. 1st and 9th (now returned to Bradley's army group) Armies, having encircled the Ruhr Valley, converged at Lippstadt and forced the surrender of 300,000 Germans. The Germans' capitulation freed the two armies to continue their advance to the east, where they took Kassel, Hannover, Leipzig, and Halle before arriving at the west bank of the Elbe River.

Meanwhile, Patton's swift-moving 3rd Army captured Bayreuth, Hof, and Plauen before Eisenhower ordered him to stop near the Czechoslovak border. Soon after receiving the order to halt his drive, Patton told Ike that they needed to drive on Berlin, arguing that he could make it there in two days. Eisenhower replied, "Well, who would want it?"[123]

Patton placed both hands on his friend's shoulders and said, "I think history will answer that question for you."[124] Surprisingly, Field Marshal Montgomery agreed with Patton.

"The Americans could not understand that it was of little avail to win the war strategically if we lost it politically," Montgomery wrote in his memoirs, convinced, as many Britons were, of the political and territorial threat of communism in the postwar world. "It became obvious to me in the autumn of 1944 [that] we were going to 'muck it up.' I reckon we did."[125] Yet at the time, perhaps because of the wide ocean separating Europe from the United

Allied tanks advance through the ruins of Nuremberg. The capture of Berlin would prove to be a politically and historically sensitive issue.

States, few Americans foresaw the potential dangers of communism.

To the southwest, while Patton held fast in anguished obedience, Lieutenant General Alexander M. Patch's 7th Army (6th Army Group) seized in quick succession Nuremberg, Munich, Berchtesgaden, and Salzburg. At the same time, the French 1st Army (also 6th Army Group) swept south to the Swiss border.

On 25 April, an American patrol from the U.S. 69th Infantry Division (VII Corps, 1st Army) met a Soviet advance guard at

"Severely Tested and Found Adequate"

Historian Stephen E. Ambrose calls infantryman Bruce Egger, of G Company, 328th Regiment, 26th Division (of Patton's 3rd Army), "representative" of the millions of GIs who served in northwest Europe. This extract from Egger's memoir of the war is included in Ambrose's *The Victors, Eisenhower and His Boys.*

More than four decades have passed since those terrible months when we endured the mud of Lorraine, the bitter cold of the Ardennes, the dank cellars of Saarlauten. . . . We were miserable and cold and exhausted most of the time, we were all scared to death. . . . But we were young and strong then, possessed of the marvelous resilience of youth, and for all the misery and fear and the hating every minute of it the war was a great, if always terrifying, adventure. Not a man among us would want to go through it again, but we are all proud of having been so severely tested and found adequate. The only regret is for those of our friends who never returned.

Torgau on the Elbe River. The East and West had met at last, and the meeting of the twain had split Germany and Kesselring's forces in two.

Three days later, Italian partisans added an ignoble period to the fascist rule that had begun twenty-three years earlier. Near the lakeside village of Dongo, they shot Mussolini, his mistress Clara Petacci, and fifteen of the former dictator's friends and associates who had been captured with him. The shootings occurred in retaliation for the killing of fifteen Italian partisans in Milan nine months earlier. The corpses of Mussolini and his mistress were taken to Milan the next day and strung upside down in public display.

Hitler, after conceding that "the war is lost,"[126] shot himself in his Berlin bunker on 30 April 1945—eighteen days after Roosevelt's death and two days after Mussolini's. Hitler left behind a last testament in which he blamed the Jews for all the ills in the world and enjoined the government and the people to continue the persecution of the Jews.

And he prophesied, "Through the sacrifice of our soldiers and my own fellowship with them unto death, a seed has been sown in German history that will one day grow to usher in the glorious rebirth of the National Socialist [Nazi] movement in a truly united nation."[127] At 2250 on the night of Hitler's suicide, the Soviets raised their flag over the Reichstag (German parliament building).

The Soviets had by then completely surrounded Berlin, and they forced the

German capital to surrender on 2 May. Had President Roosevelt lived to see the city's fall, he might have said, "Two down and one to go."

The next day, Lübeck, Wismar, and Hamburg fell to the British in the north. Elements of the 7th Army advanced through the Brenner Pass and established contact with the U.S. 5th Army moving northward from Italy on 4 May. A day later, all of the German troops in the Netherlands, Denmark, and northwest Germany surrendered to Montgomery.

On 25 April, American troops greet their Soviet comrades at Torgau. Berlin would surrender one week later.

On 7 May 1945, Germany surrendered unconditionally to General Eisenhower at Reims, France. And much of the free world celebrated VE (Victory in Europe) Day the next day.

VE Day and Another War to Win

At the cessation of hostilities, the Allies began at once to take over their assigned occupation zones in Germany and Austria, which had been agreed upon by Roosevelt, Churchill, and Stalin at Yalta, in the Crimea, during 4–11 February 1945. A cold war between the Western and the Eastern Allies was already taking shape, but what mattered most in May 1945 was that the killing in Europe had ended.

On 8 May 1945, President Harry S. Truman announced Germany's surrender to the American people. That date became indelibly engraved in the annals of world history as VE Day—Victory in Europe Day. Churchill called the German capitulation "the signal for the greatest outburst of joy in the history of mankind."[128]

Throngs of humanity in London, Paris, New York, and Moscow swept into the streets in great waves to dance and rejoice, to hug and kiss, and to share the sheer bliss of having survived to savor the moment. In Moscow, the Soviet flag hung beside the Stars and Stripes, and the rejoicing throngs roared, "Long live Truman!" "Long live Roosevelt's memory!" "Long live the great Americans!"[129]

In London, as Clare Boulter later recalled,

> The King and Queen did their balcony bit, we roared and cheered. I was intrigued by a spontaneous ceremonial on our fringe of the crowd: a very solemn group had made a bonfire and was feeding it with Green Park chairs, each one being passed from hand to hand with a bow, the last one in line placing it on the flames with courtly deliberation. . . .
>
> We departed the scene at 10.30 p.m. How I spent the rest of May 8, 1945, I can't now remember. Perhaps I couldn't even remember on May 9.[130]

Londoners celebrate the defeat of Germany. The killing in Europe ended in May 1945, but there was still a war in the Pacific to be won.

In the United States, President Truman broadcast a reminder to the American people of the tasks that lay ahead:

We must work to bind up the wounds of a suffering world—to build an abiding peace, a peace rooted in justice and law. We can build such a peace only by hard, toilsome, painstaking work—by understanding and working with our Allies in peace as we have in war.[131]

At a hunting lodge in Berchtesgaden, Private Patrick S. O'Keefe and a companion, both of E Company, 506th Regiment, 101st Airborne, encountered a German man on VE Day. O'Keefe remembered their meeting well:

He was holding himself erect but it was noticeable that he had a bad right leg. I glanced at it; he explained, "I was with the Afrika Korps and was shot up badly and sent home. I was a soldier."

Victory Message to the Troops

The route you have traveled through hundreds of miles is marked by the graves of former comrades. Each of the fallen died as a member of the team to which you belong, bound together by a common love of liberty and a refusal to submit to enslavement. Our common problems of the immediate and distant future can be best solved in the same conceptions of cooperation and devotion to the cause of human freedom as have made this Expeditionary Force such a mighty engine of righteous destruction.

Let us have no part in the profitless quarrels in which other men will inevitably engage as to what country, what service, won the European war. Every man, every woman, of every nation here represented has served according to his or her ability, and the efforts of each have contributed to the outcome. This we shall remember—and in doing so we shall be revering each honored grave and be sending comfort to the loved ones of comrades who could not live to see this day.

DWIGHT D. EISENHOWER

(Reprinted in the *Reader's Digest Illustrated Story of World War II*)

A veteran of Operation Overlord visits his fallen comrades at a cemetery near Normandy.

He asked us to come in and have a glass of wine. We said "no" but he said "Wait! I'll bring it out," and he left, to reappear with three glasses of wine. We raised them in salute, as he said, "To the end of the war." We raised ours, and we all drank. There was something basically soldierly and right about it.[132]

No one welcomed the end of the carnage in Europe more than General Bradley—one of the finest soldiers of them all—who later wrote that, since D day, 586,628 American soldiers had fallen—135,576 to rise no more. The grim figures haunted me. I could hear the cries of the wounded, smell the stench of death. I could not sleep: I closed my eyes and thanked God for victory.[133]

While there was much to celebrate on VE Day, there was also much—and many—to mourn. And the dying was not yet over. There remained another war to win in the Pacific.

★ Notes ★

Introduction: Selection of Battles

1. Quoted in Sidney C. Moody Jr. and the Associated Press, *War in Europe*. Novato, CA: Presidio Press, 1993, p. 87.

2. Omar N. Bradley and Clay Blair, *A General's Life: An Autobiography by General of the Army Omar N. Bradley and Clay Blair*. New York: Simon & Schuster, 1983, p. 167.

3. Quoted in Samuel Eliot Morison, *Sicily-Salerno-Anzio: January 1943–June 1944*, vol. 9 of *History of United States Naval Operations in World War II*. Boston: Little, Brown, 1954, p. 297.

4. Quoted in John Laffin, *Brassey's Dictionary of Battles*. New York: Barnes & Noble, 1998, p. 143.

5. Quoted in Charles B. MacDonald, *A Time for Trumpets: The Untold Story of the Battle of the Bulge*. New York: Quill, 1985, p. 35.

6. Quoted in Stephen E. Ambrose, *The Victors, Eisenhower and His Boys: The Men of World War II*. New York: Simon & Schuster, 1998, p. 327.

Chapter 1: World War II in Europe

7. Quoted in Edward Jablonski, *A Pictorial History of the World War II Years*. New York: Wings Books, 1995, p. 21.

8. Winston Churchill, *Their Finest Hour*, vol. 2 of *The Second World War*. Boston: Houghton Mifflin, 1948, p. 115.

9. Quoted in John Toland, *Adolf Hitler*. New York: Anchor Books, 1992, p. 649.

10. Quoted in Stephen E. Ambrose and C. L. Sulzberger, *American Heritage New History of World War II*. New York: Viking, 1997, p. 128.

11. Quoted in Bradley and Blair, *A General's Life*, p. 141.

12. Quoted in S. L. A. Marshall, ed., "'Operation Husky': The Sicilian Campaign," in Reader's Digest Association, *Reader's Digest Illustrated Story of World War II*. Pleasantville, NY: Reader's Digest Association, 1978, p. 332.

13. Quoted in the Editors of Time-Life Books, *WW II: Time-Life History of the Second World War*. New York: Barnes & Noble, 1995, p. 229.

14. Winston Churchill, *Closing the Ring*, vol. 5 of *The Second World War*. Boston: Houghton Mifflin, 1951, p. 488.

15. Quoted in the Editors of Time-Life Books, *WW II*, p. 237.

16. Quoted in Norman Polmar and Thomas B. Allen, eds., *World War II: The Encyclopedia of the War Years 1941–1945*. New York: Random House, 1996, p. 588.

17. Quoted in Polmar and Allen, *World War II*, p. 97.

18. Quoted in David G. Chandler, *Battles and Battlescenes of World War Two*. New York: Macmillan, 1989, p. 129.

Chapter 2: Operation Torch: The Battle for North Africa

19. Quoted in A. J. P. Taylor, *The Second World War and Its Aftermath*. London: Folio Society, 1998, p. 262.

20. Quoted in Moody and the Associated Press, *War in Europe*, p. 77.

21. Quoted in Charles B. MacDonald, *The Mighty Endeavor: The American War in Europe*. New York: Da Capo Press, 1992, p. 73.

22. Quoted in William L. O'Neill, *A Democracy at War: America's Fight at Home and Abroad in World War II*. New York: Free Press, 1993, p. 168.

23. Quoted in Taylor, *The Second World War and Its Aftermath*, p. 262.

24. Quoted in Martin Gilbert, *The Second World War: A Complete History*. New York: Henry Holt, 1989, p. 375.

25. Quoted in Karl Detzer, "Operation Torch," in *Reader's Digest Illustrated Story of World War II*, p. 302.

26. Quoted in Carlo D'Este, *Patton: A Genius for War*. New York: HarperCollins, 1995, p. 434.

27. Quoted in D'Este, *Patton*, p. 439.

28. Quoted in Gilbert, *The Second World War*, p. 378.

29. Quoted in MacDonald, *The Mighty Endeavor*, p. 114.

30. Quoted in Gilbert, *The Second World War*, p. 389.

31. Detzer, "Operation Torch," p. 307.

32. Bradley and Blair, *A General's Life*, pp. 123–24.

33. Detzer, "Operation Torch," p. 309.

34. Quoted in Moody and the Associated Press, *War in Europe*, p. 83.

35. Quoted in Moody and the Associated Press, *War in Europe*, pp. 83, 85.

36. Quoted in the Editors of Time-Life Books, *WW II*, p. 226.

37. Quoted in D'Este, *Patton*, p. 471.

38. Bradley and Blair, *A General's Life*, p. 159.

Chapter 3: Operation Husky: The Battle for Sicily

39. Bradley and Blair, *A General's Life*, p. 180.

40. Quoted in Moody and the Associated Press, *War in Europe*, p. 107.

41. Quoted in Morison, *Sicily-Salerno-Anzio*, p. 67.

42. Morison, *Sicily-Salerno-Anzio*, p. 70.

43. Quoted in Morison, *Sicily-Salerno-Anzio*, p. 70.

44. Quoted in Ambrose and Sulzberger, *American Heritage New History of World War II*, p. 341.

45. Bradley and Blair, *A General's Life*, p. 181.

46. Bradley and Blair, *A General's Life*, p. 183.

47. Gilbert, *The Second World War*, p. 445.

48. Quoted in Gilbert, *The Second World War*, p. 445.

49. Quoted in D'Este, *Patton*, p. 509.
50. Quoted in the Editors of Time-Life Books, *WW II*, p. 227.
51. Bradley and Blair, *A General's Life*, p. 193.
52. Quoted in D'Este, *Patton*, p. 533.
53. Quoted in D'Este, *Patton*, p. 533.
54. Quoted in the Editors of Time-Life Books, *WW II*, p. 227.
55. Quoted in the Editors of Time-Life Books, *WW II*, p. 227.
56. Quoted in Bradley and Blair, *A General's Life*, p. 200.
57. Quoted in D'Este, *Patton*, p. 532.

Chapter 4: Salerno-Anzio-Rapido: The Italian Campaign

58. Quoted in Morison, *Sicily-Salerno-Anzio*, p. 232.
59. Quoted in Robert Leckie, *The Wars of America*, vol. 2. New York: HarperCollins, 1992, p. 768.
60. Quoted in John C. McManus, *The Deadly Brotherhood: The American Combat Soldier in World War II*. Novato, CA: Presidio Press, 1998, p. 236.
61. Quoted in J. F. C. Fuller, "The Invasion of Italy," in *Reader's Digest Illustrated Story of World War II*, p. 335.
62. Quoted in Leckie, *The Wars of America*, p. 769.
63. Quoted in Fuller, "The Invasion of Italy," p. 335.
64. Quoted in MacDonald, *The Mighty Endeavor*, p. 215.
65. Quoted in C. B. Dear and M. R. D. Foot, eds., *The Oxford Companion to World War II*. New York: Oxford University Press, 1995, p. 574.
66. Quoted in the Editors of Time-Life Books, *WW II*, p. 230.
67. Quoted in the Editors of Time-Life Books, *WW II*, p. 232.
68. Quoted in MacDonald, *The Mighty Endeavor*, p. 224.
69. Quoted in the Editors of Time-Life Books, *WW II*, p. 232.
70. Quoted in Leckie, *The Wars of America*, p. 789.
71. Quoted in MacDonald, *The Mighty Endeavor*, p. 235.
72. Quoted in Ambrose and Sulzberger, *American Heritage New History of World War II*, p. 358.
73. Quoted in the Editors of Time-Life Books, *WW II*, p. 235.
74. Quoted in Moody and the Associated Press, *War in Europe*, p. 119.
75. Quoted in Moody and the Associated Press, *War in Europe*, p. 119.
76. Quoted in Ambrose and Sulzberger, *American Heritage New History of World War II*, p. 362.

Chapter 5: Operation Overlord: Normandy

77. Quoted in Kenneth S. Davis, "Overlord: The Allies' Triumph in Normandy," in *Reader's Digest Illustrated Story of World War II*, p. 348.
78. Quoted in Leckie, *The Wars of America*, pp. 794–95.
79. Leckie, *The Wars of America*, p. 795.
80. Quoted in Moody and the Associated Press, *War in Europe*, p. 127.

81. Cornelius Ryan, *The Longest Day: June 6, 1944.* New York: Simon & Schuster, 1959, pp. 135–36.

82. Quoted in Stephen E. Ambrose, *D-Day, June 6, 1944: The Climactic Battle of World War II.* New York: Simon & Schuster, 1994, pp. 277–78.

83. Quoted in Ambrose, *D-Day, June 6, 1944*, pp. 278–79.

84. Quoted in Ambrose, *D-Day, June 6, 1944*, p. 274.

85. Quoted in Ambrose, *D-Day, June 6, 1944*, p. 274.

86. Quoted in Ryan, *The Longest Day*, p. 8.

87. Quoted in Ambrose, *The Victors, Eisenhower and His Boys*, p. 93.

88. Quoted in Jon E. Lewis, ed., *Eyewitness D-Day: The Story of the Battle by Those Who Were There.* New York: Carroll & Graf 1994, pp. 127–28.

89. Ryan, *The Longest Day*, pp. 208, 225.

90. Quoted in Moody and the Associated Press, *War in Europe*, p. 130.

91. Quoted in Moody and the Associated Press, *War in Europe*, p. 131.

92. Quoted in Moody and the Associated Press, *War in Europe*, p. 131.

93. Quoted in Leckie, *The Wars of America*, p. 800.

94. Quoted in Michael D. Doubler, *Closing with the Enemy: How GIs Fought the War in Europe, 1944–1945.* Lawrence: University Press of Kansas, 1994, p. 10.

Chapter 6: The Ardennes: The Battle of the Bulge

95. Quoted in Stephen E. Ambrose, *Citizen Soldiers: The U.S. Army from the Normandy Beaches to the Bulge to the Surrender of Germany: June 7, 1944–May 7, 1945.* New York: Simon & Schuster, 1997, p. 355.

96. Quoted in Ambrose, *Citizen Soldiers*, p. 354.

97. Quoted in the Editors of Time-Life Books, *WW II*, p. 316.

98. Quoted in the Editors of Time-Life Books, *WW II*, p. 317.

99. Quoted in Bradley and Blair, *A General's Life*, pp. 350–51.

100. Quoted in Bradley and Blair, *A General's Life*, p. 349.

101. Quoted in Bradley and Blair, *A General's Life*, p. 350.

102. Quoted in Ambrose, *Citizen Soldiers*, p. 198.

103. Quoted in the Editors of Time-Life Books, *WW II*, p. 318.

104. Quoted in the Editors of Time-Life Books, *WW II*, p. 322.

105. Quoted in John Toland, *Battle: The Story of the Bulge.* New York: Random House, 1959, p. 77.

106. Quoted in Toland, *Battle*, pp. 193–94.

107. Quoted in Toland, *Battle*, p. 263.

108. Quoted in Toland, *Battle*, p. 263.

109. Quoted in Frank Conniff, "'Thus Far—and No Farther' in the Bulge," in Jack Stenbuck, ed., *Typewriter Battalion: Dramatic Frontline Dispatches from World War II.* New York: William Morrow, 1995, p. 276.

110. Conniff, "'Thus Far—and No Farther' in the Bulge," p. 277.

111. Quoted in Polmar and Allen, *World War II*, p. 99.

Chapter 7: Remagen and the Race to Berlin

112. Quoted in Moody and the Associated Press, *War in Europe*, p. 173.
113. Quoted in Charles B. MacDonald, *The Last Offensive*. New York: Konecky & Konecky, 1973, p. 215.
114. Quoted in Ken Hechler, "The Capture of the Remagen Bridge," in *Reader's Digest Illustrated Story of World War II*, p. 403.
115. Quoted in the Editors of Time-Life Books, *WW II*, p. 338.
116. Quoted in Bradley and Blair, *A General's Life*, p. 407.
117. Quoted in Polmar and Allen, *World War II*, p. 513.
118. Quoted in Polmar and Allen, *World War II*, p. 513.
119. Quoted in Gerald F. Linderman, *The World Within War: America's Combat Experience in World War II*. New York: Free Press, 1997, p. 104.
120. Quoted in Gilbert, *The Second World War*, p. 664.
121. Quoted in Moody and the Associated Press, *War in Europe*, p. 178.
122. Quoted in Gilbert, *The Second World War*, p. 662.
123. Quoted in D'Este, *Patton*, p. 721.
124. Quoted in D'Este, *Patton*, p. 721.
125. Quoted in D'Este, *Patton*, p. 721.
126. Quoted in Moody and the Associated Press, *War in Europe*, p. 180.
127. Quoted in Gilbert, *The Second World War*, p. 677.

Epilogue: VE Day and Another War to Win

128. Quoted in Ambrose and Sulzberger, *American Heritage New History of World War II*, p. 559.
129. Quoted in Ambrose and Sulzberger, *American Heritage New History of World War II*, p. 559.
130. Quoted in Martin Gilbert, *The Day the War Ended: May 8, 1945—Victory in Europe*. New York: Henry Holt, 1995, p. 200.
131. Quoted in Ambrose and Sulzberger, *American Heritage New History of World War II*, p. 561.
132. Quoted in Stephen E. Ambrose, *Band of Brothers: E Company, 506th Regiment, 101st Airborne: From Normandy to Hitler's Eagle's Nest*. New York: Simon & Schuster, 1992, pp. 280–81.
133. Quoted in O'Neill, *A Democracy at War*, p. 388.

★ Glossary ★

Allies: The Allied countries of World War II; principally, Britain, France, the Soviet Union, and the United States.

Axis: The Axis countries of World War II; chiefly, Germany, Italy, and Japan.

blitzkrieg: Lightning war.

CCS: Combined (Anglo-American) Chiefs of Staff.

chancellor: The chief minister of state in some European countries.

DUKW: A six-wheeled boat-shaped truck, named for its factory designation (D = model year, U = amphibian, K = all-wheel drive, W = dual rear axles); nicknamed the "Duck."

Festung Europa: Fortress Europe.

führer: Leader.

Higgins boat: See LCVP.

Kampfgruppe: Battle group.

La drôle de guerre: The Phony War; six-month period of inactivity in Western Europe at the beginning of World War II.

LCI: Landing craft, infantry (USA).

LCT: Landing craft, tank (USA).

LCVP: Landing craft, vehicle/personnel (USA); often called Higgins boat (after its creator).

lebensraum: Living space.

LST: Landing ship, tank (USA).

Luftwaffe: German air force.

National Socialist German Workers' Party: The Nazi Party, or NSDAP, from *National-sozialistische Deutsche Arbeiterpartei.*

Nazi: A member of the National Socialist German Workers' Party.

panzer: Tank.

Reichstag: German parliament; also parliament building.

RN: Royal Navy.

SHAEF: Supreme Headquarters, Allied Expeditionary Force.

strategy: The plan for an entire operation of a war or campaign.

Stuka: A gull-winged German dive-bomber (Junkers Ju-87).

tactics: The art of placing or maneuvering forces skillfully in a battle.

Treaty of Versailles: The 1919 peace agreement that ended World War I.

Tripartite Pact: The mutual-defense treaty signed by Germany, Italy, and Japan on 27 September 1940.

USA: U.S. Army.

USN: U.S. Navy.

VE Day: Victory in Europe Day, 8 May 1945.

Waffen-SS: The military arm of Heinrich Himmler's *Schutzstaffel,* or Elite Guard.

Wehrmacht: German army.

West Wall: The Siegfried Line; the fortified defensive line along Germany's western frontier.

✯ Chronology of Events ✯

1939

1 September: Germany invades Poland; World War II begins.

27 September: Fall of Warsaw.

1940

9 April: Germany invades Denmark and Norway.

10 May: Germany invades Luxembourg, Holland, and Belgium.

26 May–4 June: British Expeditionary Force evacuates from Dunkirk.

5–25 June: Fall of France.

10 June: Italy declares war on Britain and France.

10 July–31 October: Battle of Britain.

1941

22 June: Germany invades the Soviet Union (Operation Barbarossa).

8 September–27 January 1944: Siege of Leningrad.

9–23 September: Battle of Kiev.

8 October–30 April 1942: Battle of Moscow.

7 December: Japan attacks Pearl Harbor.

8 December: Japan declares war on United States and Britain.

11 December: Germany and Italy declare war on the United States.

1942

12–22 May: Battle of Kharkov.

25 June: Eisenhower assumes command of all U.S. troops in Europe.

1–27 July: First Battle of El Alamein.

23 July: Fall of Rostov.

23 August–2 February 1943: Battle of Stalingrad.

23 October–4 November: Second Battle of El Alamein.

8 November: Allies invade Morocco and Algeria (Operation Torch).

17 November–13 May 1943: Battle of Tunisia.

1943

14–22 February: Battle of Kasserine Pass.

23 April: Anglo-American headquarters established in Britain to plan invasion of Europe.

5–17 July: Battle of Kursk.

10 July–17 August: Battle for Sicily (Operation Husky).

5 August: Soviets drive toward Dnieper River, the last major German defensive line in Soviet territory.

9–18 September: Battle of Salerno (Operation Avalanche).

22 September: Soviets establish first bridgehead across Dnieper.

1 October: Naples falls to Allies.

12 October–14 November: Battle of the Volturno River.

7 November: Soviets liberate Kiev; German

defenses on Dnieper start collapsing.

20 November: Allies strike across Sangro River in Italy.

24 December: Eisenhower named supreme Allied commander for the invasion of Western Europe.

1944

16 January: Eisenhower assumes duties as supreme Allied commander in Europe.

17 January–22 May: Battle of Cassino.

22 January–23 May: Battle of Anzio (Operation Shingle).

27 January: Soviets oust Germans from Leningrad.

10 April: Soviets regain Odessa in Ukraine.

9 May: Soviets retake Sevastopol.

4 June: Allies liberate Rome.

6 June: D day; Allies land in Normandy (Operation Overlord).

7 June–25 July: Battle of Caen.

22 June: Soviets begin Operation Bagration (massive summer offensive).

25 July: Allies commence Normandy breakout.

13–19 August: Battle of Argentan-Falaise Pocket.

15 August: Allies land in southern France.

25 August: Allies liberate Paris.

30 August–28 October: Gothic Line Campaign.

17–25 September: Battle of Arnhem (Operation Market Garden).

2 October: Allies breach West Wall into Germany.

4 October–1 December: Battle of Aachen.

20 October: Soviets and Yugoslav partisans take Belgrade.

16 December–28 January 1945: Battle of the Bulge.

1945

17 January: Soviets occupy Warsaw.

19 January: Germans in full retreat along eastern front.

8 February: Allies launch major offensive to reach Rhine River.

7–31 March: Battle of Remagen and the Rhine crossings.

7 April: Soviet troops enter Vienna.

12 April: Roosevelt dies; Harry S. Truman becomes president.

16 April–2 May: Battle of Berlin.

25 April: Americans and Soviets meet at Elbe River.

29 April: German forces in Italy formally surrender.

30 April: Hitler commits suicide in Berlin.

7 May: Germany formally surrenders.

8 May: VE Day.

☆ For Further Reading ☆

Robert W. Black, *Rangers in World War II.* New York: Ballantine Books, 1992. The story of the elite group of warriors who led the way at Normandy and beyond.

William B. Breuer, *Drop Zone Sicily: Allied Airborne Strike, July 1943.* Novato, CA: Presidio Press, 1997. The baptism by fire for Allied airborne troops.

Tom Brokaw, *The Greatest Generation.* New York: Random House, 1998. The story of a generation of American citizen heroes during World War II.

Paul Carell, *Invasion—They're Coming! The German Account of the Allied Landings and the 80 Days' Battle for France.* New York: E. P. Dutton, 1963. The Normandy landings and aftermath from a German perspective.

David G. Chandler et al., *Chronicles of World War II.* Godalming, UK: Bramley Books, 1997. Selected accounts of great campaigns.

Christopher Chant, ed., *Warfare and the Third Reich: The Rise and Fall of Hitler's Armed Forces.* New York: Smithmark, 1996. A detailed assessment of Hitler's military power.

Don Congdon, ed., *Combat World War II Europe: Unforgettable Eyewitness Accounts of the Momentous Military Struggles of World War II.* New York: Galahad Books, 1996. Stirring accounts of combat life.

Carlo D'Este, *Decision in Normandy.* New York: HarperCollins, 1994. One of the best researched and best written histories of the Normandy invasion.

James F. Dunnigan and Albert A. Nofi, *Dirty Little Secrets of World War II: Military Information No One Told You About the Greatest, Most Terrible War in History.* New York: William Morrow, 1994. Interesting infobytes of little-known aspects of military operations.

Samuel Hynes, *The Soldiers' Tale: Bearing Witness to Modern War.* New York: Viking, 1997. Illuminates the nature of war in the twentieth century.

Kathleen Krull, *V Is for Victory: America Remembers World War II.* New York: Knopf, 1995. Memorabilia honoring the fiftieth anniversary of the Allied victory.

Judy Barrett Litoff and David C. Smith, *We're in This War, Too: World War II Letters from American Women in Uniform.* New York: Oxford University Press, 1994. The first comprehensive account of uniformed women in the Second World War.

STRATEGIC BATTLES IN EUROPE

Don McCombs and Fred L. Worth, *World War II: 4,139 Strange and Fascinating Facts*. New York: Wings Books, 1996. A compendium of more than four thousand entries on the people, battles, and events of World War II.

David Miller, *Great Battles of World War II: Major Operations That Affected the Course of the War*. New York: Crescent Books, 1998. Riveting tales of epic land, sea, and air battles.

Edward F. Murphy, *Heroes of World War II*. Novato, CA: Presidio Press, 1990. Capsule biographies and descriptions of World War II heroics.

Studs Terkel, *"The Good War": An Oral History of World War II*. New York: New Press, 1990. A compelling, dramatic, and interesting collection of tales of those who fought the battle.

James Tobin, *Ernie Pyle's War: America's Eyewitness to World War II*. New York: Free Press, 1997. A telling biography of America's favorite war reporter.

Flint Whitlock, *The Rock of Anzio, from Sicily to Dachau: A History of the U.S. 45th Infantry Division*. Boulder, CO: Westview Press, 1998. A fine history of one of the U.S. Army's great infantry divisions.

★ Works Consulted ★

Stephen E. Ambrose, *Band of Brothers: E Company, 506th Regiment, 101st Airborne: From Normandy to Hitler's Eagle's Nest.* New York: Simon & Schuster, 1992. The author captures the essence of a rifle company.

———, *D-Day, June 6, 1944: The Climactic Battle of World War II.* New York: Simon & Schuster, 1994. Packed with the dramas and horrors of the Normandy landings.

———, *Citizen Soldiers: The U.S. Army from the Normandy Beaches to the Bulge to the Surrender of Germany: June 7, 1944–May 7, 1945.* New York: Simon & Schuster, 1997. A gripping account of the Second World War.

———, *The Victors, Eisenhower and His Boys: The Men of World War II.* New York: Simon & Schuster, 1998. Soldiers' stories drawn from five of the author's books.

Stephen E. Ambrose and C. L. Sulzberger, *American Heritage New History of World War II.* New York: Viking, 1997. A masterful updating of the standard reference work.

Omar N. Bradley and Clay Blair, *A General's Life: An Autobiography by General of the Army Omar N. Bradley and Clay Blair.* New York: Simon & Schuster, 1983. A frank narrative of the general's life.

David G. Chandler, *Battles and Battlescenes of World War Two.* New York: Macmillan, 1989. Concise accounts of fifty-two of the war's most important battles.

Winston Churchill, *Their Finest Hour.* Vol. 2 of *The Second World War.* Boston: Houghton Mifflin, 1948. Portrays England's early struggles during World War II.

———, *Closing the Ring.* Vol. 5 of *The Second World War.* Boston: Houghton Mifflin, 1951. Recounts the war from Guadalcanal to the eve of the Normandy assault.

C. B. Dear and M. R. D. Foot, eds., *The Oxford Companion to World War II.* New York: Oxford University Press, 1995. A one-volume masterwork on the greatest war in history.

Carlo D'Este, *Patton: A Genius for War.* New York: HarperCollins, 1995. A revealing portrait of a complex and controversial military personality.

Michael D. Doubler, *Closing with the Enemy: How GIs Fought the War in Europe, 1944–1945.* Lawrence: University Press of Kansas, 1994. Explains how the GI quickly learned to become a formidable fighting man.

Ernest Dupuy and Trevor Dupuy, *The Encyclopedia of Military History: From 3500 B.C.*

to the Present. Rev. ed. New York: Harper & Row, 1986. The definitive one-volume work on military history.

Editors of Time-Life Books, *WW II: Time-Life History of the Second World War.* New York: Barnes & Noble, 1995. A condensation of Time-Life's thirty-nine-volume series.

Desmond Flower and James Reeves, eds., *The War, 1939–1945: A Documentary History.* New York: Da Capo Press, 1997. A huge anthology of war stories and reportage.

Juliet Gardiner, *D-Day: Those Who Were There.* London: Collins & Brown, 1994. The people's story of D day.

Martin Gilbert, *The Second World War: A Complete History.* New York: Henry Holt, 1989. Total history of the global war by a master historian.

———, *The Day the War Ended: May 8, 1945—Victory in Europe.* New York: Henry Holt, 1995. An entertaining account of one of the most celebrated days in history.

Edward Jablonski, *A Pictorial History of the World War II Years.* New York: Wings Books, 1995. A highly readable pictorial treatment of World War II.

John Laffin, *Brassey's Dictionary of Battles.* New York: Barnes & Noble, 1998. Brief accounts of conflicts, campaigns, and wars spanning thirty-five hundred years.

Robert Leckie, *The Wars of America.* Vol. 2. New York: HarperCollins, 1992. A comprehensive narrative of American wars from 1900 to 1992.

Jon E. Lewis, ed., *Eyewitness D-Day: The Story of the Battle by Those Who Were There.* New York: Carroll & Graf, 1994. The real story of the battle by those who fought it.

Library of America, *Reporting World War II, Part Two: American Journalism 1944–1946.* New York: Library Classics of the United States, 1995. An anthology of war reporting by some of America's finest reporters.

Gerald F. Linderman, *The World Within War: America's Combat Experience in World War II.* New York: Free Press, 1997. A tale of fighting men and what makes them tick.

Charles B. MacDonald, *The Last Offensive.* New York: Konecky & Konecky, 1973. Follows four U.S. armies in their sweep across Germany during World War II.

———, *A Time for Trumpets: The Untold Story of the Battle of the Bulge.* New York: Quill, 1985. Exhaustively researched and splendidly told story of the battle.

———, *The Mighty Endeavor: The American War in Europe.* New York: Da Capo Press, 1992. One of the best one-volume books of America's war in Europe.

John C. McManus, *The Deadly Brotherhood: The American Combat Soldier in World War II.* Novato, CA: Presidio Press, 1998. Tells what the battle experience was like for American combat soldiers and marines.

Charles Messenger, *Sepp Dietrich: Hitler's Gladiator, the Life and Times of Oberstgruppenführer and Panzergeneral-Oberst der Waffen-SS Dietrich.* London: Brassey's, 1988. An objective account of Hitler's favorite warrior.

Edward G. Miller, *A Dark and Bloody Ground: The Hürtgen Forest and the Roer River Dams, 1944–1945.* College Station: Texas A&M University Press, 1995. Small unit actions set against the sometimes senseless acts of high command.

Sidney C. Moody Jr. and the Associated Press, *War in Europe.* Novato, CA: Presidio Press, 1993. A profusely illustrated and compelling narrative of the war.

Samuel Eliot Morison, *Sicily-Salerno-Anzio: January 1943–June 1944.* Vol. 9 of *History of United States Naval Operations in World War II.* Boston: Little, Brown, 1954. Still the definitive account of the title campaigns.

William L. O'Neill, *A Democracy at War: America's Fight at Home and Abroad in World War II.* New York: Free Press, 1993. A highly perceptive examination of the weaknesses and shortcomings of a democracy at war.

Norman Polmar and Thomas B. Allen, eds., *World War II: The Encyclopedia of the War Years 1941–1945.* New York: Random House, 1996. The definitive resource on the war from an American perspective.

Reader's Digest Association, *Reader's Digest Illustrated Story of World War II.* Pleasantville, NY: Reader's Digest Association, 1978. A collection of stories that together tell the tale of World War II.

Cornelius Ryan, *The Longest Day: June 6, 1944.* New York: Simon & Schuster, 1959. Still the best story of the men of the Allied forces at Normandy.

Jack Stenbuck, ed., *Typewriter Battalion: Dramatic Frontline Dispatches from World War II.* New York: William Morrow, 1995. War correspondents report from the war front in World War II.

C. L. Sulzberger, *World War II.* New York: American Heritage, 1985. A treatise on the war, written in an engrossing style for the lay reader.

A. J. P. Taylor, *The Second World War and Its Aftermath.* London: Folio Society, 1998. The war on the battlefronts and behind the scenes.

John Toland, *Battle: The Story of the Bulge.* New York: Random House, 1959. Exciting, detailed, fast-reading account of one of the war's most famous battles.

————, *Adolf Hitler.* New York: Anchor Books, 1992. An insightful biography of the man behind World War II.

Peter G. Tsouras, *Warriors' Words, a Quotation Book: From Sesotris III to Schwarzkopf, 1871BC to AD1991.* London: Arms and Armour Press, 1992. Interesting vignettes and quotations about and from men at war.

☆ Index ☆

★ Picture Credits ★

Cover photo: Digital Stock

Archive Photos, 12, 16, 17, 18, 21, 26, 30, 37, 42, 46, 62, 65, 66, 67, 71, 76, 95, 99 (both), 103, 105, 106, 108

Brown Brothers, 91

Corbis, 9, 13 (bottom), 34, 40, 49, 50, 52, 54, 55, 74, 78, 80, 87, 89, 90

Corbis/Hulton-Deutsch Collection, 23, 24, 32, 39, 48, 58, 61, 81, 84, 107

Corbis/Michael Maslan Historic Photographs, 53

Corbis/Bettmann, 7, 10, 13 (top), 25, 28, 69, 82, 92

Digital Stock, 5, 11, 15, 20, 98, 101 (top)

FPG International, 45, 59, 63, 64, 75, 97

Imperial War Museum, 35

Lineworks, Incorporated, 57

National Archives, 14

pixelpartners, 33, 68, 79, 83, 101 (bottom)

Popperfoto/Archive Photos, 96

Martha Schierholz, 29, 41, 70, 85

★ About the Author ★

Earle Rice Jr. attended San Jose City College and Foothill College on the San Francisco peninsula, after serving nine years with the U.S. Marine Corps.

He has authored more than thirty books for young adults, including fast-action fiction and adaptations of *Dracula, All Quiet on the Western Front,* and *The Grapes of Wrath.* Mr. Rice has written seventeen books for Lucent, including *The Cuban Revolution, The Salem Witch Trials, The Final Solution, Nazi War Criminals, Life in the Middle Ages,* and seven books in the popular Great Battles series. He has also written articles, short stories, and miscellaneous website materials and has previously worked for several years as a technical writer.

Mr. Rice is a former senior design engineer in the aerospace industry who now devotes full time to his writing. He lives in Julian, California, with his wife, daughter, two granddaughters, two cats, and a dog.